the Art of
LEADERSHIP

ENGAGING FAMILIES

IN EARLY CHILDHOOD ORGANIZATIONS

Exchange Press, Inc.

17725 NE 65th Street • B-275

Redmond, WA 98052

(800) 221-2864 • www.ChildCareExchange.com

THE ART of LEADERSHIP

Engaging Families in Early Childhood Organizations

The Art of Leadership series replaces the popular Exchange Press textbook, *The Art of Leadership: Managing Early Childhood Organizations.* The entire series demonstrates the great complexity of an early childhood leader's job. Each volume expresses the importance of one aspect of this role. Each leader will need to prioritize all these roles based on many factors, including the skills that reside within the members of his team.

These articles were originally published in *Exchange Magazine.*
Every attempt has been made to update information on authors and other contributors
to these articles. We apologize for any biographical information that is not current.
Exchange is a bimonthly management magazine for directors, owners, and teachers
of early childhood programs. For more information about
Exchange and other Exchange Press publications for directors and teachers, contact:

Exchange Press, Inc.
17725 NE 65th Street • B-275
Redmond, WA 98052
(800) 221-2864 • www.ChildCareExchange.com

ISBN 978-0-942702-59-0

Printed in Korea by Four Colour Print Group, Louisville, Kentucky

© Exchange Press, Inc., 2016

Cover Design: Cover Painting by Fons Heijnsbroek
(https://flic.kr/p/g2yfXa) licensed under CC BY 2.0

the *Art of*
LEADERSHIP

ENGAGING FAMILIES
IN EARLY CHILDHOOD ORGANIZATIONS

Introduction

Chapter 1: Welcoming, Engaging, Supporting Parents

Chapter 2: Communicating with Parents

Chapter 3: Working with All Types of Families

Empowering Parents

by Jim Greenman

"Get real! I think parents are already too powerful! They want this and that for their kids, as if their child was the only child in the center. They will want to have a say on curriculum, on fees, on everything. If I ask what they think, or worse let them decide, all hell will break loose."
Director responding to an earlier article on parent partnerships (*Exchange*, November, 1998)

It's easy for those us who are not in the daily thick of things to talk and write about the value of full parent partnerships — empowering parents. We can be confident in our wisdom, generous in our knowledge, and charitable in our recognition that partnerships take work. But it's not us who are being asked to install a phonics curriculum in the twos group, lower tuition, promise that a baby will be held most of the time, use all organic products, serve more foods that children will eat like hot dogs, or keep their little boy out the high heels and chiffon dresses that he likes so much. But, as with empowering children or teachers, empowering parents is a vital part to creating a community of caring and learning.

So with full recognition that reality is a lot more real in the office than on the page, what follows is all about empowering parents and what it means to adopt a model of full partnership.

What Exactly is Full Partnership?

Partnerships are about sharing power. Parent involvement, parent information, parent education, and friendly relationships are usually elements important to establish or maintain partnerships, or the outcome of parent partnerships. Information is not input and both are very different than influence. Input may or may not result in any real partnership. If my input doesn't lead to my having influence (actually as important: my feeling influential), I'm not going to believe a partnership exists.

A full partnership between a family and the child care center means that a family will have significant influence over their child's experience at the center: his or her care and education. A full partnership with families means that parents, as a group, can have significant influence on the center's operations that determine the experience children have at the center including curriculum issues, allocation of resources, parent policies. A parent will feel influential as an individual and also feel that parents can be influential.

So Mr. Parent-lover, you ask, what exactly does significant influence mean? It means what you say it means: and the proof whether it exists is in the pudding, whether, in fact, parents feel empowered! Every center has to define the parameters of the potential partnership, the possibilities for individual and collective influence, based on your goals, your approach, and your ownership or sponsorship. The reality check is whether a parent actually feels influential.

A critical point: having the opportunity to influence and feeling influential doesn't necessarily result in parents trying to wield power. Knowing that my voice will be heard, that my opinion counts, that I will be consulted on important issues, doesn't turn me into a power-hungry tyrant or noxious gadfly, more likely the opposite. I don't need to exert it because my partnership is assumed. I may choose to use my power because I like working with the center and joint decision-making, or my child's experience is not good and the center inspires no confidence, or perhaps because I am a power-hungry jerk (see boxes).

Jerks Will Be Jerks

In child care, as with any other intensive service, it's easy to create theys and thems out of parents. "They don't listen." "They don't respect us." And we use the parent who doesn't ever listen, or the parent who acts like an egotistical prima donna as prime examples of 'they' when we are trying to restrict information or influence. But, almost all of the parents listen most of the time, and very few parents are full-time or even part-time jerks. The fact that jerks will be jerks, fools will be fools, and rigid people will be rigid, shouldn't be a factor in structuring relationships with parents (or teachers, or directors, or any other group of people).

Why Empower Parents?

Schooling in America provides an example of a model of very limited partnership and parent power — usually only the power to become upset and try and block initiatives. The result: complaints, dissatisfaction, blame, and limited understanding. Parents need power in child care because:

- **Ideology:** We expect parents to assume responsibility for the care and education of their children and hold them accountable for raising a good child. We are their support system.

- **Better care and education:** When parents are full partners, each child is more likely to receive better care and education, consistent with family values; even if curriculum includes compromises that the program accepts with reluctance.

- **Support for center efforts:** Partnership creates allies and the center will run more effectively.

- **Better child futures:** Sending parents off to the world of school with expectations of partnership and advocacy for their child is great for children and the schools.

What's the alternative? Involving parents in decision-making removes from the director the need to play God and be the font of all wisdom. Why take sole responsibility for decisions that will prove divisive? Late policies, field trip charges, holiday celebrations, and some curriculum decisions can be discussed. Many decisions have issues where there is no consensus; they involve balancing the needs and desires of the community. There is no one right answer, and acceptance of the decision is as important as the decision — certain curriculum issues, for example. Often the best course is to assume responsibility for defining the criteria for the decision, and the range of solutions that the center can accept, and working toward some consensus.

Parents as Customers and Partners

Partnership and parent power is not incompatible with considering parents as clients or customers. As with any business or service, our job is to meet customer needs and create satisfied customers. Does this mean that we can't have standards and values that sometimes place the program's views of the child's needs or program needs over the parents' wishes? Or that we can't stick to our guns about some policies and practices? Of course not. Just as a conscientious craftsman or doctor won't pander to customers against their own expert judgments, neither should we. It does mean, however, that the foundation of our service is serving customer needs. It is in our interest to define, and sell our product — that is, what we believe quality child care and education are all about — in a way that parents understand. Satisfied parents who feel good about their child's care are a fundamental ingredient in child care quality. Keys to empowering parents as customers are:

- **We define the product:** Developmentally appropriate, NAEYC accreditation-quality care, Montessori education, or early academics or whatever we articulate as our program.

- **We define the market:** Who are our customers? High- or low-income families, a particular community, a particular workforce?

- **Concerns, criticism, and ideas are legitimate and necessary:** We want to know what families think. We solicit opinions and are pleased when we receive unsolicited ideas and opinions. We understand that customers are the lifeblood of our business: They pay our salaries and secure our future. They are not people to argue and match wits with.

What Power Should Parents Have?

The power to know: Parents have the right and the responsibility to know: the program goals; philosophy; expectations for children, families, and staff; operating assumptions and practices that will accomplish the goals; and how resources are allocated to achieve goals. (The more you feel you can share about the economics of your situation and the more parents have to connect up the dots and recognize that child care is an inherently expensive operation, the less mistrust and potential ill will). The power to ask: Can my child do this, or not do that? Could I have this flexibility? What is the thought behind that policy and is it necessary?

The power to be upset: There are lots of reasons to get upset in the intense real world of sharing care. Things get overlooked, lost, communications fail, bites materialize, fees get raised, hopes are deflated,

and all the other irritants and wounds that child care life creates. Note that the power to be upset is not the same as the power to take that upset out on others.

The power to question why: As a parent responsible for my child's well being, I need the power to question to do my job. Objections should lead to a process of trying to reconcile disagreements.

The power to decide together: I need the power to have the option of deciding together on those things that matter most to me — within the boundaries established by the program.

Power that Parents Should Not Have

The power to block: Life must go on and sharing power means moving ahead to reconciliation.

The power to dictate: Partnership is working together and reaching shared decisions.

The power to disrupt or be disrespectful: If the center is going to function as a community, no one should have the power to disrupt or be disrespectful to others — children or adult. When it happens, and people will lose it at times in the intimate and intensive world of child care, there should be a clear cultural assumption that apologies and amends are in order.

Building Partnerships

Empowering Parents Through Organizational Structures and Systems

Individual parents are empowered through:

- primary caregiver systems that assume parent communication and family advocacy as a primary caregiver role.

- multiple information vehicles that include notes, journals, conferences, documentation panels, displayed planning forms and objectives, web pages, and meetings.

■ teacher training and support that empowers teachers to be competent, confident partners.

Reasons Not to Empower Parents?

Are there situations where empowerment is not a good idea? Empowering parents requires good leadership: in particular, maturity, confidence, and very good communication skills. It also helps to have a program that has the makings of a community where parents are open to working together. You are in for trouble if:

■ you are unable to overcome your fear and defensiveness.

■ you are unable to articulate your center's mission and approach.

■ many parents don't like or trust you.

■ you have counted and you feel that you do have a disproportionate number of jerks, fools, and malcontents. (If the number is higher than 10%, you might want to ask why this is so and if no reason is apparent — check your criteria and your behavior.)

■ you are afraid of empowering teachers. Teacher empowerment goes hand in hand with parent empowerment.

Empowerment through a Culture of Partnership

Culture is a powerful medium, one of the basic organizational dimensions that create and maintain quality. (The others are the environment; organizational structures, systems, and routines; and human resources.) Good companies and centers, like all good organizations, have cultures that shape how its members think, feel, and behave. Centers that empower parents have a cultural philosophy of:

We are all in this together.

Who is the 'we'? Teachers, support staff, cooks, accountants, administrators, our sponsor, and the parents and children.

What is the this? Raising children, supporting working parents and families, creating a great place to work, making the world a better place.

What does together mean? Collaboration, shared decision-making, shared expectations, shared responsibility.

■ We are all in this together to support families and help children become lifelong learners, achieve literacy, and become prepared for success in school and life.

■ We are all in this together in times of individual and group crisis: such as child biting, difficult separations, faculty turnover, difficult transitions, family distress, or other center challenges.

■ We are all in this together balancing tuition cost to parents, faculty compensation, cost to clients, and return on investment.

■ We are all in this together in making a difference to all the children and families of the community in which we live and work.

Why not?

Why not defines a key way of thinking at a center that empowers children, parents, and faculty and encourages creativity and individualized, personalized responses. When a parent or teacher (or even a child) asks for something (e.g. special care, a change in policy), the first thought is why not do what we are asked to do, instead of why?, or no because "we don't do that here." BUT, why not does not mean yes. There are many legitimate why-nots that lead to a no to parents (or teachers, or children): a practice may be harmful to a child (for example, bottles of juice in the crib, spanking), the center budget, the complexity of group life may not allow it, caregivers don't know how, and staffing situations to name a few. The program has no reason to be defensive about unalterable givens that lead to our limitations.

The why-not approach does something very powerful: it legitimizes the right to ask the question, forces the program to constantly be thinking, and gives the center the benefit of more creative thinking. This is different from a customer is always right approach.

The outcome of a why-not approach is not unmanageable chaos, but thoughtful care, a foundation of mutual respect, and in most cases, increased trust that we are professionals thinking through good care. Equally important, a why-not approach leads to innovation and better care. Parents and teachers bring to light important questions and concerns, and share their expertise. Parents acting as informed consumers fulfill their responsibility to ensure their children have the care they deserve.

Let's figure it out.

Many problems involve balancing different perspectives, tradeoffs with less desirable side effects, and creative solutions. A let's figure it out culture recognizes:

- I (director, teacher) don't have to have all the answers.

- Daily life in child care is complicated and requires thoughtful problem-solving and problems are often solved by a 'we' and 'us' taking responsibility, not 'you' or 'I'.

Empowerment is a Developmental Journey

Empowerment is not all-or-nothing. There is a continuum ranging from parents feeling out of the loop to actually running the place. Partnerships vary in breadth and depth and will be different with each family. They take work and grow over time. In practice, partnership with families requires a continual exchange of communication. In the process, parents learn a lot about child development and curriculum, and the center learns about what parents feel is important for their children to grow up to be the kind of people they expect them to be. Full parent partnerships that recognize and respect the common

bonds and the ways that families and children are different build a community of caring and learning.

Jim Greenman

Jim Greenman dedicated more than 30 years to the early childhood field as an educator, early childhood administrator, and author. Throughout his career, he worked with employer-sponsored, inner city, hospital, and university programs; early childhood and family education programs; Head Start; family child care; and public and private schools. Jim played a significant role in the facility and program design process for more than 100 early childhood projects, taught at the Institute on Child Care Design at the Harvard Graduate School of Design, and was senior vice president for education and program development at Bright Horizons Family Solutions. He held a master's degree from the University of California at Berkeley, where he also completed additional advanced graduate courses. Jim passed away in 2009 after a courageous battle with cancer. He inspired many people in the early childhood field through his dedication and work in the early childhood field; Jim's legacy leaves an ever-lasting gift to children and educators.

the Art of
LEADERSHIP

ENGAGING FAMILIES
IN EARLY CHILDHOOD ORGANIZATIONS

CHAPTER 1
Welcoming, Engaging, Supporting Parents

Making Families Welcome

by Deadru Hilliard

For anyone who enters the center, our goal is for them to see that parents and families are valued in our program. We want them to come away with a feeling that if they had children this is where they would like them to be, and that they feel honored referring us to others. Parents and families play a very vital role in the classroom because they are children's first teachers. Children observe and interact with others in ways that have been modeled for them, mostly by their parents. When new families enter into our class, there are a number of ways that we try to make them feel welcome.

Initial Contact

Our main goal is to learn about the child. We ask parents to come in and talk with us about their child. We allow them to find out if we fit their needs and to get an overview of what the center is all about. We ask what it is they need from us other than child care. This may be their first encounter with someone asking them to think more in-depth about what they want for their child. They may be dealing with leaving their child for the first time, so we spend the first half-hour just talking. We ask them to share some insights about their family and to elaborate on what expectations they have.

Many times parents can feel rushed about having to choose a space in a short period of time. When we talk with them and share knowledge about this experience, they then begin to gather their thoughts and give us their perspectives. We ask them to look at the many different ways in which other programs do things, starting with something as simple as watching how our staff and other centers' staff operate, before making a choice. We talk about the community within the classroom where families come together and how the tone is set and partnerships are established. It can be the beginning of a trusting relationship, and in some cases, a lifelong bond.

Relationships Built between Parents and Staff

As we thought about rearranging our classroom, we came up with an idea of putting adult-size chairs around the different play areas. They are used to invite parents in to sit and talk with teachers or to observe children in their play. Parents are encouraged to give us feedback about their observations or any suggestions about the room. Interaction with parents and other children also happens during this time, allowing for families to form new relationships and community.

When enrolled in the center, new parents are introduced to all staff from the director to the kitchen manager. Each staff member plays a key role in how well the center is maintained. Parents become familiar with all of those who come in contact with their child as well as those who spend a major portion of their day with that child. Parents can utilize any staff person to gain resources and information, even when their child's teacher is not present. This establishes a commitment to work together and with their child so that all transitions to the next level go well.

Parents are taken in to talk with the lead teacher of the class where they get to see just how parents are represented. They begin their conversations once again around the child and talk about what their values and goals are. There is a specific requirement we have of parents on the first day their child begins and that is to spend one hour of class time with us. We want parents to feel comfortable in their choice and utilize this time to ask questions and start a connection with teachers and other staff.

Representation of Parents

Once we go over schedules, lesson plans, signing in and out, and other center requirements, parents are given a tour of the class. There are many displays and boards that represent families. They speak of what their hopes and dreams are, what they see in their child, and ask how we can help. We offer the chance to reflect on what parents themselves wanted to be when they were growing up and in what ways their child mirrors them.

Framed photos of families are brought in and placed throughout the room on shelves, countertops, and in children's areas of play. As you watch you will see children engage in conversation with other families while learning about identity.

Another of our mini-activities includes parents creating display boards that best describe their child's world. Through pictures and open-ended materials, parents come up with elaborate designs that give children a positive image of themselves.

What I have learned by having parents do these projects is that: 1) the experience gives us a chance to engage like old friends sharing our stories; and 2) it allows us to sustain our commitment to work with each other and collaborate together. In parents' busy everyday lives they sometimes fall into the habit of just picking up their child out of routine. Parents need to know that they are valued and that we commend them for the job that they do every day for their child, making a continuous effort to provide and take care of their families. Our conversations are not always about unwanted behavior or filling out paperwork. They also consist of talking about current events of the world or sharing stories about one's family and having the connection from adult to adult. Sharing a bit of ourselves can open parents up to talk about difficult issues and concerns, or to just ask for those necessary resources that they may feel uncomfortable going into detail about. We assure them that we chose to be an extension of their families and we will go the distance to help them succeed, all the while caring for their child.

Once we have established a relationship, parents find themselves losing track of time because they come in and we begin to talk and share. It's not that they don't have other things to do, but there are times when these genuine and authentic moments of communication just happen.

When sharing with parents, I try and give them as much information to work with as possible. They are as efficient and capable as we are, but their day can be filled with lots of events that they have not had the time to deal with. Our mission statement not only speaks to children, but is inclusive of parents in creating internal growth for them, too.

Communication

Keeping the lines of communication open with parents can be done in many ways. Some parents call throughout the day and some use the computer to receive information through e-mail. Others leave notes or pass questions on to the staff person who is there when they arrive or leave. We have a board that is set up for this particular task. If a parent leaves a note for me while I'm out of the building, other staff transfers information onto the staff board under my name. It is then our job to check for any messages and return any calls necessary. We don't want to miss the chance to help in whatever way we can, because parents may lose their comfort in asking and the relationship can become distant.

Parents who don't know one another use our parent meetings, potluck luncheons, and yearly celebration times to get better acquainted. We don't want these events to be the only time they talk, so our job then becomes how to keep them connected. One of the ways I like to do this is to ask for a parent's permission to share information or insights with other families and for them to be open as resources if possible. Their children also assist in this by talking about their day and sharing what goes on throughout the classroom. Parents become familiar with children's names and begin to ask us who they are so that there is a face to place with the name. This allows both children and adults to begin to explore new friendships outside of class.

We find out many different things about one another in these gatherings. It benefits us all when we come together and talk about children, work, and life itself. Asking families continuously for feedback about the things that work for them and what does not, helps us maintain our commitment to them. We want our environment to reflect all of those whom we serve. Giving parents this strength and power now will help them become even stronger advocates for their children when they transition out of the center and into other learning institutes.

Deadru Hilliard

Deadru Hilliard has been working at Martin Luther King Day Home Center in Seattle, Washington, for just over 11 years. She has been working hard to continuously grow in this profession and at the same time empower parents. In addition to that, her future studies include working with other early learning teachers just entering the field and providing them with a solid foundation right at the start.

Redefining Parent Engagement

An Interview with Mary Jo Deck

by Margie Carter

This summer I read a terrific little book by Michael Gramling (2015), *The Great Disconnect in Early Childhood Education: What We Know vs. What We Do*. I highly recommend it to anyone trying to figure out why publicly-funded ECE programs have not successfully addressed the achievement gap for children living in poverty. In the foreword to the book, Elizabeth Jones points out:

"The gap between rich and poor children in America hasn't narrowed, as promised; it has widened. Public funding backfired. Preschools funded for the poor are caught in the canned curriculum and testing mania. The preschool experiences of privileged children are more likely to be developmentally appropriate (building on what all recent research now verifies) than are preschool experiences of young children who start out behind — and fall further and further behind…. Early intelligence grows through choices and complexity and self-esteem and negotiating with others — not through memorizing prescribed lists of facts."

Along with his mates at Defending the Early Years (DEY, see References below), Gramling outlines some key problems that have led to the current trends in ECE, especially those programs targeting children in low-income families.

Much to the detriment of young children, the establishment of school readiness standards has caused the early childhood profession to:

■ equate instruction with assessment.

■ confuse child development with early learning.

■ substitute early information for early experience.

Examining Bias

While I think many early childhood professionals recognize these problems in publicly-funded early childhood programs, Gramling's adds a call to examine the bias, and oftentimes blaming tone, inherent in the parent education component of these programs. He reminds us that for parents in poverty, "much of everyday life is consumed with trying to figure out how to accomplish simple daily tasks that people with money take for granted." And Gramling reminds us that these challenged parents, often seen as deficient, actually provide excellent role models for resourcefulness, critical thinking, and problem solving.

I've been eager to find efforts that counter this deficit view with a re-conceptualized notion of 'parent education.' There are voices challenging this bias on social media. Searching the web you will discover a

PHOTOVOICE

Shenekia McDaniels: The shoes are this week's theme. That was the picture that I took; I put a clock in the middle, because I never have enough time. I took a picture of everyone's shoes who depend on me putting my shoes on properly. Everybody puts their shoes together except for Kalia; I only found one of them, but I said I am taking this picture because I don't have time to come back for this. So, that's a little clock, my son's shoes, my niece's shoes, and my momma's shoes who all depend on me putting my shoes on properly.

variety of terms to replace 'parent education': family engagement, family involvement, family partnerships, and parent empowerment.

We have professional literature reminding us that when families are involved in their children's schools, children are more likely to succeed. But parents will often tell you that the tone embedded in the call for parent involvement is frequently off-putting, rather than inspiring parents to bring their funds of knowledge to help shape their child's education.

Changing how we traditionally approach our work with parents is a challenging and complex task, especially given the ever-growing inequities and mistrust across the economic and racial divides in our country. What are some of the structures, supports, and strategies that show promise for strengthening the agency and voice of families in poverty?

A Dialogue with Mary Jo Deck

At the end of an informal social gathering with early childhood professionals in North Carolina, I found myself next to Mary Jo Deck who was describing her NC Shape work project with Smart Start of Buncombe County, funded to promote healthy weight in young children and help families lead healthier lives. Mary Jo described using "PhotoVoice" for this project, a qualitative research method designed to capture individuals' voices and visions about their lives, the community, and concerns through photographs taken by participants. PhotoVoice projects (see References) often bring together specific populations who are marginalized or who don't have a strong voice. I was vaguely familiar with this work in another context, but had never come across it in our field. In the course of my late-night probing, Mary Jo eagerly described the adaptation of this approach for her Smart Start project:

"Participants in a PhotoVoice project are equipped with cameras and work on a weekly photo assignment that is meaningful for them. The groups meet for 4-6 weeks to share and discuss the photographs they have taken. All sessions are led by a trained facilitator and notes are transcribed and reviewed later by a team for research purposes. At the end of the project, participants decide how to present their stories and identify an actionable community change.

MC: My immediate thought is that the PhotoVoice project is a terrific way to level the playing field and avoid some of the disempowering aspects of other approaches to helping low-income families.

MJD: Yes, I think it starts with the idea that we can begin to listen, to ask parents questions about their roles as parents and their needs for specific assistance in that role, and acceptance of where they are now. For this project, we have partnered with the Positive Parenting Program to explore a variety of issues and challenges of parenting. Our participants are primarily parents with children at The Asheville City Schools Preschool. It is an ethnically diverse group of women: some are single mothers, some are married, some live in public housing, some have one child and others have four children.

In our six weeks of photo assignments we explored:

■ the many challenges to keeping your children healthy and safe.

■ how long and tiring the days are.

■ how moms felt judged and stereotyped.

■ how living in poverty makes it all harder.

MC: As you describe these themes that emerged, I'm thinking you must have introduced this project in a different way to get to the real issues in the parents'

PHOTOVOICE

Sarah Copeland: I took a picture of the snacks that my son enjoys eating and the snacks that I try to get him to move towards. *How is that working for you?* Not great. We have outside impacts, for instance the brownies and PopTarts came from my mom. The Girl Scout Cookies came from the neighbor's child who came over and said, "You have to buy Girl Scout Cookies from me," and then the Sponge Bob snacks are something we use sparingly, or at least I attempt to. And then the apples and bananas are the things I try to get him to eat as often as possible.

lives. Quite often programs focused on families in poverty predetermine what help they think parents could benefit from, rather than creating a way for the parents to name that for themselves.

MJD: We began thinking about this with exposure to a webinar highlighting the classic elements of Photo-Voice. At the time, we were working on community needs assessments and knew that we wanted a more genuine conversation with parents in order to inform programming and policy, and how to empower parents to be active participants in decision making.

As we talked with a variety of diverse community programs about their own approaches to genuine parent involvement, it became clear that most struggled to fit parents into roles and activities that matched their own program needs. This is very different than honest dialogue.

Working together with Deanna LaMotte of the Positive Parenting Project and the Preschool, we met with a large group of parents, shared our purpose, and explained the project. This included the number of people to be involved, how to use a camera, how many weeks the project would last, and an agreed upon schedule. A very important part of the orientation was the clear articulation of the central fact that the story is the parent's story told through photographs, and parents own it and decide what they want to do with it.

MC: As the process unfolded, I imagine you discovered the difference between being a parent educator and being a facilitator of a group of parents.

MJD: Oh, it is very different! Listening allows you to really hear and understand that the experience of parenting has some universals, and that race, education, and economics are powerful dividers. The PhotoVoice process, with the camera or without, offers an open-ended opportunity for parents to talk openly about their lives, share with one another, and educate us. What participants choose to photograph not only brings a theme and detail of a story to the group, but then it frames the conversations and questions that result, offering a clear guide to additional issues that the group has in common.

As the conversations weave in and out of stories and feelings, parents will share what they need, what works and what doesn't. We laugh and share common experiences. For instance, one of the elements highlighted was a series of photos of routine household responsibilities. There are laundry pictures, laundry baskets, both woven fiber and plastic, overflowing; socks and shirts hanging out of dresser drawers; and sinks piled with dirty dishes. This was totally spontaneous, and four of the six women recorded it. I still remember seeing the first laundry basket photo and I laughed aloud!

MC: What a bonding experience that must have been, between the women themselves, but also between you and them. To be a facilitator in a setting where one already has more power and privilege — perhaps through education, skin color, or more financial security — requires that we unlearn some attitudes

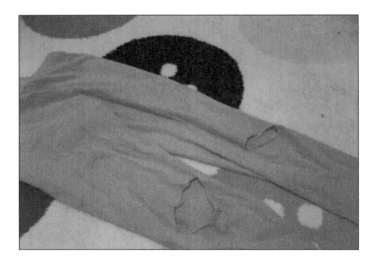

PHOTOVOICE
Polly Bolding: This is a piece of clothing that my child loves, but I'm worried about someone seeing her in these horrible, falling apart leggings and having them think that we are not setting appropriate limits or paying attention to how she takes care of herself or looks. At the same time, she really loves these leggings and I am not sure if I want to have a power struggle about the leggings. Or I guess I am not confident about that limit because she likes wearing the leggings and a part of my mind thinks, "It's not a big deal"; but the other part of my mind says, "Well, what if other people think it is a big deal?"

and behaviors if we are to be allies, partners, and true collaborators. What have you learned about this?

MJD: I am honored to be a part of this open and honest conversation. We must dispense with our preconceptions and stereotypes and ask and listen. Listen longer. I believe that sharing the stories builds a bond, a community of parenting. When we name the subjects and objects, for example, grocery shopping with young children with a crying incident and the resulting looks and stares of disapproval from other shoppers. If we pull back the curtain of shame or embarrassment or unease, then we can collectively address what we want to do about it — perhaps finding ways to prevent a temper tantrum in the cereal aisle of the grocery store.

I believe that honesty and willingness to be vulnerable and ask for help, along with the power of shared experience and mutually creating an identified plan of action, is the basis for hope.

MC: Any final thoughts you'd like to share with our readers?

MJD: Over the months of this project there are several clear lessons that will continue to impact our work of community engagement. The first is that really giving parents a place — a kitchen table is the description that comes to mind — to share their own stories and needs and dreams for their children is a way for them to discover their own part of the universe of parenting and find their uniqueness and special gifts in that role. Participants in the PhotoVoice project own what they have shared, they decide how and with whom they want to share their photos and their words, and they discover there is individual personal power there.

Another lesson is that PhotoVoice allows and supports a genuine sense of the shared experience of parenting in which children grow. There were times when each of us held our breath as one mom talked about a particularly painful experience, and we didn't really know how to respond except to listen and nod and know that all we had to offer was the sense of shared understanding. Issues of racial prejudice and economic disparities are powerful negatives that were brought into the conversations. When this happened, suddenly our own biases about these realities were exposed and our preconceptions become empathetic awareness. Then there were other moments when both individuals and the group laughed aloud for long moments when we recognized ourselves in the situation.

All along the way the sharing was powerful. And allowing the stories of these everyday occurrences to inform and guide genuine parent involvement and create a bridge of universal understanding was an important and real benefit. We've been able to put our PhotoVoice exhibit of the parent voices on our website. (Details for accessing it are listed in the References.)

Perhaps the final lesson to acknowledge here is the opportunity for each of us to be personally changed by the experience. We can move to a new understanding and acceptance. With an honest letting go

PHOTOVOICE
Shenekia McDaniels: That's my son climbing the stairs; just like it is a climb up, you really have to work hard and so many things — so many connections — have to be made to climb out of poverty. So many resources, so I thought, "Okay, the steps can be the resources that you would have to use in order to get yourself up out of poverty."

PHOTOVOICE
Shenekia McDaniels: And then there is the fish tank; I thought, "Look at the fish. They look so free and they have no care or worry that they're trapped in this little box." (People laughing.) So I thought, "That's kind of what being in poverty is. It's like you're swimming around. You're making it look good, but there is a limit to where you can go because of what you need to come out of there, and the needs and the assistance to get out of the position that you're currently in."

of some 'standards' about parenting, we enter a place of honoring the work of raising the future generation.

As a result of the success of using the PhotoVoice project to redefine parent engagement, we have received support from the Asheville City Schools Foundation to continue using PhotoVoice with parents, teachers, administrators, and children to explore racial equity. This relates directly to the Gramling reference at the beginning of this article: looking at the benefits of parent involvement when we create opportunities for families to construct a role and have a voice in publicly-funded preschools.

References

Defending the Early Years:
http://deyproject.org/recommended-reading-and-resources/

Gramling, M. (2015). *The great disconnect in Early Childhood Education. What we know vs. What we do.* St Paul: Redleaf Press.

Photo Voice:
www.photovoice.org/

Smart Start of Buncombe County Guidebook: Keeping our children healthy and safe and the challenges of parenting: A PhotoVoice Exhibit. Online:
www.smartstart-buncombe.org/images/linkeddocs/photovoiceguidebook.pdf

Margie Carter

Margie Carter is the co-founder of Harvest Resources Associates (www.ecetrainers.com) and the co-author of numerous books and early childhood videos. As she moves towards retirement years, her professional work is focused on highlighting and supporting the inspiring work of new leaders and uplifting the voices and leadership of teachers in the field.

Mary Jo Deck

Mary Jo Deck, MS, currently works in North Carolina as Community Engagement Specialist with Smart Start of Buncombe County, which includes facilitating the PhotoVoice project. A seasoned early childhood education consultant, Mary Jo founded Staurolite Resource Group, a firm dedicated to supporting systems change through the development of personal and organizational learning. She has directed both small, private parent cooperative model preschools and large multi-site Head Start programs. Currently a North Carolina C Environmental Educator, Mary Jo's current passion is focused on playing and learning in the outdoors.

Helping Children and Families Develop a Sense of Belonging

by Donna King

Every early childhood program has its own aspirations for the children and families it serves:

- Maybe you care most that children make friends and resolve conflicts peacefully.

- Maybe your passion is helping children and their families connect with the natural world.

- Perhaps you hope children will claim and master many expressive languages to make their ideas and imaginings visible to themselves and others.

- You may be committed to helping every child gain competence and confidence in early academics: writing, reading, and counting.

Whatever it is you hope to achieve, your success will depend on how fully you are able to help each child and family develop a sense of belonging in your program. To learn is to risk and to venture — and most of us won't risk and venture unless we feel fundamentally secure where we are. We must feel that we are on the 'inside' of someplace safe in order to step outside of ourselves and grow.

So how, as the people already inside, do we open our programs fully to the people we serve? How do we create a culture in our programs that ensures each member of the community will feel a sense of belonging?

Here's what I heard when I posed this question to some of the parents, teachers, and children who have been part of our program.

Welcome Me

"We felt welcomed immediately. You made us feel welcome with just the simple things like making a point of saying 'Hello' and asking 'How are you?' every morning. It felt like you really wanted to know how we were; it wasn't just the 'polite' thing to do." — Mikele, parent

"It's very easy to get friends here. Because people like you the minute you walk in. Even if they don't really, really like you, once you're really in there, they still do like you. And you don't even need to be nice to them. They just say, 'Hi.' I remember that it was easy to get into the school." — Noah, age 5, reflecting back on starting school when he was 3.

Whenever and however you first meet the children and families who will become your children and families, you have the opportunity to help them feel welcome:

■ Do you have a system for matching incoming families with 'buddy families' for play dates before school begins?

■ At program open houses, are there plenty of teachers and parents there with smiles, handshakes, and greetings?

■ When you host visitors, is their presence announced on your morning message board?

■ Do you let current families know who is coming, so they will be prepared to introduce themselves?

"To know that not only are people willing to have you in their circle but happy to have you, is a gift." — Susan, parent

See Me

"Moving from outside to inside has to do with being received in some way. . . . Reception that involves attention and acknowledgment of who you are. The people on the inside show an interest in how you experience the world and particularly this place we share together. Respect is embedded in the concept of welcome." —Margie, parent

"An absolute commitment to seeing and appreciating kids as individuals. I think recognizing each person is fundamental to a sense of belonging." — Kristin B. B., parent

When you orient new families, do you focus on things you want them to do: finish the paperwork, send extra clothes, sign in and out? Or do you use this opportunity to launch the profound work of seeing that child and family with clarity and appreciation?

This is the time to ask families about their hopes and dreams, their challenges and vulnerabilities, their fierce beliefs and their deep questions. You are setting the tone for a new relationship of meaningful collaboration.

And in the weeks and months and years after orientation — each time we write an e-mail, compose a newsletter, put together a required form, sit down for a parent conference, document learning for a child's portfolio, or ask about the weekend — through our tone and our choice of words, we have the opportunity to say it again: "I see you, in all your particularity, and you are more than an interchangeable part of this place."

"Here's how you make friends. You learn their names." — Niko, age 4

"With four children over 9 years, it would have been easy (and frankly, natural) for the children to be 'Berlin-Schulmans' but that was not the case. They were Jake, Eli, Micah, and Becca and they were each seen, each time, with fresh eyes and complete acceptance." — Brenda, parent

It begins with names. Ask people what they would like to be called: Beatrice or Bee or Bea? Sarah, or Miss Sarah, or Ms. Meyer? Post photos with names in a prominent place so that people have support in learning to put faces and names together. Find ways to make a project for children of learning ALL the names — not just the children, but their parents and siblings, too. Consider name quizzes in mailboxes, photo matching games, and lunchtime conversations about family names.

Show Me

"When you walk in you begin to know you are being encouraged to be in the world with sensitivity, caring, support, and beauty. This is a world that encourages community as well as allowing for individual exploration. The environment says, 'Yes!' It feels like all things are possible, and it does not take long to want to

be there, to want to join, to leave the outside and come inside." — Kristin, parent

"There is external evidence that you belong here. When you first come, there are pictures of yourself and your family all over the school. Your needs are anticipated. And there is a transparency about what's expected. 'Can I find my way around? Can I make sense of this place? Do I know what different parts are for? Is there someone to guide me if I can't?' I can look around and figure out what to do and that gives me a sense of agency."
— Margie, parent

Crafting the environment offers countless opportunities to create a culture of belonging. An environment that is orderly, beautiful, and comfortable invites confident engagement, the feeling that, "I know what to do here, so I belong here."

An environment with spaces and materials that children and families can claim for their own — mailboxes, coat hooks, snack cups and bowls — establishes ownership.

And prominently displayed photos of children and their families say it most clearly of all: "This is your place."

Give Me Time

"It was very strange at first, but as the year goes by you feel that it's kind of like your home." — Andy, age 5

"Like you could just take your time making friends. You don't have to do it straight away." — Alena, age 4, offering advice in a Welcome Book

"Well, the way I did it was just make a friend, one at a time. One step at a time. That's how

I did it." — Oliver, age 4, reflecting on how to make friends in a Welcome Book

"'Feeling on the inside' to me means that I felt completely accepted for who we are as a family. That I could talk to any parent or teacher in the community without the awkwardness of being guarded, so as not to say something that may offend somebody. . . . So I was a little scared of being my complete self, at least until I figured out how this magical community worked so well and how I could contribute to it. That took a long time." — Mikele, parent

"The image that comes to my mind here is of a little kid shyly peeking out from between the fingers of both hands, which are covering her eyes: she's watching, she is taking it all in, she wants to see, she needs to know that she can do it at her pace . . . and that whomever she's interacting with will wait patiently and not dismiss her presence just because she is not fully 'in' yet. How could she be, all at once?"
— Judy, parent

Take a hard look at structures in your program that rush or abbreviate relationships. The more time a group of children, teachers, and families are together, the better. Show patience, communicate consistently, and radiate a steady confidence that everyone will surely make their way to the inside. This lays the path to belonging.

Accept Me

"I believe that a large part of feeling that you belong starts with the feeling of being accepted for who you are. I never felt judged and I never felt that my children were being judged."
— Paula, parent

"The key to feeling a true sense of belonging and moving from the outside to the inside has to do with a feeling that you are . . . not only accepted, but valued and appreciated for all of who you are." — Khristine, parent and teacher

"I remember you telling us before we enrolled: 'If Niko were to bite another child, he doesn't become an anonymous biter. We talk openly about this stuff.' This put me at ease, knowing that we were all in it together and could trust in the community to work together on whatever came up, as best we could."
— Kristin B. B., parent

"I love my school so much and I want to kiss it. . . . Because it's a safe school, that's all."
— Max, age 4

In some ways, it is simple. If you want to make your program a safe and accepting place, you simply say it, over and over: "This is a safe place, and I won't let you hurt anyone here, and I won't let anyone else hurt you, either." And then there are subtler strategies that communicate acceptance:

- Inviting families and children to be open about their challenges and difficulties.

- Generously using the phrase 'still learning' when those challenges present themselves.

- Approaching families as soon as you think something may be wrong — especially when you suspect they are unhappy with you or the program: "I'm not completely sure what to do, but I have some ideas, and we'll figure it out together."

Put Me to Work

"You don't get a sense of belonging from being catered to. You get it from contributing to the community. You belong when you feel connected through action of some kind (playing together, working together, a cause, a task). There has to be meaningful exchange for true belonging. A valuable part of the experience is the invitation to give of yourself."
— Margie, parent

"I help almost everybody in the school. I help them if they fall down; I would help them get back up. If someone gets hurt, I go over and see if they need anything. I think the nicest thing the teachers do is, they're like, 'Seth could you please go down there and rescue that ball?' The nicest thing is when they just ask me to help." — Seth, age 5

In a community, everybody pitches in. If children are to feel competent and valued, they need to do real work every day: put away blocks, wash the paint brushes, fetch a washcloth for an injured friend. It's equally important to match families with tasks that are satisfying for them and genuinely important to the functioning of your program. Give parents some ideas about what you need, and ask what they can do: web page, fence repair, legal advice, laundry? Hold your first Saturday workday early in the year so that families can connect as they work beside each other moving mulch, weeding a garden, or painting outdoor blocks. Then take advantage of ongoing opportunities for shared labor.

"What makes a good school is clean-up time, so you can learn to cooperate." — Sam, age 5

Help Me

"How some people meet their friends is by, once you get to school, somebody might help you with something and they might become your new friend. Friends play with you. Friends help you when you need help. Friends do a lot of stuff to make you feel like you've always been there." — Anna Grace, age 5

"It wasn't until the immense outpouring of support that our family received after my father died, that I really felt like an insider. The amount of love and care that every family showed for us sent me the message loud and clear: we were loved, we were supported. These actions really felt like they came from the heart . . . from the strong will to help one another in time of need." — Mikele, parent

When you belong, you know who and how to ask for help. You trust that if you are hurt or upset, someone will stop and check on you and offer aid. When you belong, you know people will listen when you speak, and they trust you to listen, too. You feel surrounded by what we call 'the caring conspiracy.'

Inform Me

"Just saying 'Hi, I'm gonna be your friend' is not okay. You have to agree with the other person. You can't just tell them to be your friend." — Susanna, age 5, offering advice in a Welcome Book

When you give prospective families clear, complete, and unapologetic information about your program — emphasizing your high expectations for family involvement and the principles and policies you will not compromise — they know what they are getting into from the beginning. When a family makes an informed choice, they are on their way to belonging. After the choice is made, a steady flow of information keeps the path to belonging clear. For children, you can provide a "Welcome Book," a collection of photographs and words from teachers and children outlining routines, introducing spaces and materials, and even explaining rules — all in a tone that balances genuine excitement about the opportunities ahead with an acknowledgment of how tender and scary it can feel to be new. Families will need plenty of written information, including clear instructions about required paperwork — but also something more

playful, like an invitation to work with their child on pages for the program's "Family Book."

Allow Me

"We feel we belong when we are allowed agency, and share power. When you belong, you are part of a story." — Margie, parent

"Belonging is not only about being accepted for who you are (or worse, tolerated for your particularity or 'difference'), but really being valued for the way you add to and transform the collective." — Laura, parent

How does your program change from day to day and year to year in response to the actual people who inhabit it? For both children and their families, a sense of belonging comes from making an impact:

- Children see their work displayed with care.

- Children watch their friends act out their dictated stories, knowing that later all the families will be reading those same stories at home via e-mail.

- Parents claim a territory or a task — the compost, the flower garden, shelving books — and get public acknowledgement for what they contribute.

- Families see the odds and ends they donate to 'creation station' end up as fancy spaceships and baby food and magic wands.

How visible is the history of your program and the ways it has been shaped over time by individual children, parents, and teachers?

Celebrate Me

"The feeling that you are welcome and respected — celebrated, even — happens in layers and deepens over time." — Susan, parent

"Belonging comes through thoughtful rituals that include parents. By having families create important presents, and including us in special days, not as spectators but as singing participants." — Ilene, parent

Ritual is a powerful and versatile tool for creating a culture of belonging. Carefully consider the occasions you choose to celebrate. Do your rituals clearly reflect your values? Do they deepen people's connection to those values and their connection to each other? We love birthdays as an opportunity to:

■ hear stories from families about things their child has learned over the years.

■ invite the birthday child to name ambitions for the future.

■ ask everyone else in the community to reflect on what they especially appreciate about the birthday child.

We treasure our December "Stone Soup Feast" as an opportunity to pause and celebrate this moment when we know we have evolved from being new to each other to being, as a favorite song puts it, "Friends of the Family." And we embrace our end-of-year Graduation Celebration as one last chance to celebrate each child's unique contributions to our community and to express our absolute belief in their potential to make the most of whatever comes next.

Inspire Me

"And of course, belonging is about the way being with others in the collective transforms you." — Laura, parent

"I remember the very first meeting where you asked us what we wanted for our children (all huddled up in a small space together). This made me feel like we were going to take a preschool parenting voyage together — and it was going to be a fun trip!" — Ilene, parent

"I feel a sense of belonging when I am invited to be my best self." — Sarah, parent and teacher

Inspiration happens where your intention to create a culture of belonging meets up with the broader purpose of your work:

■ Why should someone want to identify with this place and belong here?

■ What in your program speaks to the best in people?

■ How does your program invite people to identify and reach for their own highest aspirations?

"I said it the first day and will say it again: I wish I could stay here forever." — Kristin, parent

"I'm not a preschooler. I'm a Children Firster!" — Jack, age 4

Donna King

In 1990, Donna King, informed by her graduate school study of child care quality, worked with a group of teachers and parents to found Children First, a small, nonprofit early education program in Durham, North Carolina — and she has been teaching, directing, and, most of all, learning there ever since. She has three children — Cara, Anna Grace, and Josh — all graduates of Children First.

Developing Meaningful Relationships with Families

by Margie Carter

This fall during a staff in-service day at one of the child care centers where I do staff training, I was struck by the frustration the staff were expressing about the children's parents. Phrases like "They just don't!" and "We need to make them!" were uttered again and again. There were concerns about neglect of the children's grooming and health care, the number of hours the children were left at the center beyond the parents' work shift, the lack of communication about important information, and inconsistent follow through with behavior management.

As I listened, it occurred to me that the tone of negativity and urge toward punitive consequences was something we have worked hard to overcome in our interactions with children. I pointed this out to the group, acknowledging that these might be instinctive reactions, but as professionals we've learned to replace judging and labeling children with efforts to understand the source of their behavior.

Rather than punish, we seek to help children with their self-awareness, skill development, expressions of respect, and negotiating know-how. When we learn to sharpen our looking and listening, and cultivate a disposition of respect and curiosity towards children, we find ourselves learning and improving our relationships with them. Isn't this what parents deserve from us as well?

A number of other discussions took place on this in-service day. As things were drawing to a close, I asked the staff to each think of an individual professional goal they wanted for themselves this school year and, in addition, to develop a group goal for their program, something they wanted their center to become known for in our city. To my delight, the collective goal they chose was to improve their relationships with the children's families. This coming year they will try a number of things, drawing on their own ideas, professional resources, and things that have shown merit in other programs.

Strategy:
Create Family-friendly Environments

Take time to look around your center from the perspective of a rushed or tired parent, uncle, or grandmother. When we did this at the above-mentioned center, we realized the first thing a family encountered when they entered the building was the smell of the children's bathroom. While they begin to develop a longer-range plan to move the bathroom door to another wall away from the entryway, the staff is considering other more welcoming sites and smells to greet families at the door. Adding some plants, a potpourri with pleasant herbal scents, and an attractive display of children's art can immediately change the feel of the entryway. Already they have changed the lighting and softened up the vestibule with new paint on the walls, a new carpet, loveseat, comfy chair, and coffee table. This creates a transition space for the children and their families, one that invites lingering and a moment of conversation.

Inside the classrooms, there also need to be spaces for adults to sit comfortably. Early childhood teachers understand the importance of sitting on the floor and with the children at their low tables. However, this is hardly appealing to a tired parent and not conducive to taking time for a relaxed greeting or an exchange of information. Couches, stuffed chairs, plants, and soft lighting go a long way toward making child care rooms feel more family friendly. And how about an occasional tea party with snacks prepared by the children for their families at the end of the day?

Strategy:
Focus on the Family during
Phone Calls and Center Tours

A typical interaction with a prospective parent finds the director trying to market the program by offering lots of information about how things are done at the center. Even if the parent seems primarily concerned about the cost and hours of the program, our focus can be to explore who the child is and what is most important to their family life. Getting a sense of this requires thoughtful questions and attentive listening so that we don't appear to be prying or conducting an interrogation.

Whether in an initial phone call or during a tour of the center, our message should be that we want to know each child and family so that we can find the best way to grow their hopes and dreams. When initial conversations focus on building a relationship, rather than taking care of business, we lay the foundation for an ongoing partnership. Inquiries can include things like "Tell me a bit about your child. What kinds of things does she like to do, seem eager for, or hesitant about? What have you noticed about how she goes about learning new things, meeting

new people, or making a new friend? How does she tend to handle her feelings when she's excited, angry, or sad? Are there things you would like our help with in working with your child?"

Strategy:
Supplement Enrollment Forms
with Pages for Family Books

When a family decides to enroll their child in our program, it's common for them to be inundated with required paper work. What if we first offered them some simple pages to fill out together as a family to become part of our classroom family book? Encourage the family to complete a page together about the child and their family life and to use photos, the child's drawings, written or dictated words. You can put simple phrases in large spaces or geometric shapes on a page for these. For instance, the child's page might include her name and birthday and then things like:

■ how I got my name.

■ what I look like.

■ something I love to do.

■ something I want to learn.

■ what makes me happy.

■ what makes me sad or mad.

The family page could have prompts like:

■ who's in our family.

■ something special about each person in our family.

■ something we like about where we live.

■ someone our family admires and talks about.

■ favorite story we tell in our family.

As these pages are brought to the center, the child can help put them in the "Our Families" notebook binder that is kept close to the classroom entryway, by the couch, or wherever parents might linger with their child or other family members to read it.

Home visits are an invaluable tool for building relationships between teachers, children, and their families, but the obstacles preventing this are numerous. Creating family notebooks for the classroom can be a substitute or companion tool for these visits.

Strategy:
Invite Family Members to Share Stories of Their Childhoods

One of my favorite parts of Vivian Paley's book *The Girl With the Brown Crayon* is how she includes families in the life of her kindergarten classroom. It's common for child care and Head Start programs to request that parents share something about their culture or holiday celebrations with their child's class, but Paley does something that feels less fraught with problems. She asks family members to tell the children a story about their own childhoods.

Children love hearing stories about when adults were children, and most adults have a favorite story to share. This storytelling doesn't require any special supplies, expenditure, or particular talent, which makes it accessible for the participation of all family members, even visiting aunties or grandparents. Hearing these stories helps teachers get to know more about the families and furthers the bond between the children and their own families. xStories about their families also create new interest and friendships between the children themselves.

Strategy:
Rethink Parent Meetings

What would it take for parents to look forward to an evening in your center, rather than to make excuses or just feel obliged to attend? Low parent turnout is a chronic issue and discouragement for child care programs; we need to take a hard look at what we could be doing differently. Providing child care and food is

a good starting place, but let's also reconsider how we use the time.

I've heard several success stories that seem worth trying. One program offers a monthly meeting on learning skills such as "Using the Internet," "Cooking Thai Food," "Financial Planning and Investments," and "Tracing Your Family Tree." They develop a menu of choices at the beginning of the year from family surveys of interests and skills. Shifting from an exclusive focus on parenting skills brought more family involvement. As the monthly gatherings became popular, interest eventually cycled back to requests about parenting topics.

Another program revived an interest in parent meetings by having the children develop letters to entice their families to come. They set the date and put out the notice "Come See What Your Child Wants You To Do." Over the days leading up to the meeting, the teachers worked with the children to identify what they would like their families to discover and do in their classroom. They then developed letters, drawings, and photographs with instructions from each child on how they would like their family to spend their time at the meeting. These were kept in the classroom, but word about them went home.

When the family arrived for the meeting, they were shown their child's message and sent off to explore as instructed. The teachers took photos and jotted down notes, just as they do with the children. After a while they had a discussion as a group about the kinds of things the children are learning when they engage in these activities. Families wrote letters to their children, and these were left in the classroom along with their block structures, paintings, and photographs for the children to discover the next day.

Families at this center are eager to know when the next meeting will take place.

Strategy:
Make Memory Books and Videos

As we enter the 21st century, there is a huge emphasis on early literacy, getting kids ready for school, and maintaining standards with outcomes and bench-marks defined for different ages. The early childhood profession has been responding with calls for developmentally appropriate practice, but we have also been getting on this runaway train with an increasing emphasis on elaborate portfolio assessments and individualized learning systems. If we are basing our programs on a childhood rather than school model, I think our task is to focus more on creating memory books and videos, documenting learning through photos and stories, rather than checklists that end up on the floor of the car.

Programs I know who are doing this are asking families to donate three rolls of film or a blank video or writable CD when they turn in their enrollment papers. With prices coming down on digital cameras and voice recognition software improving, the regular creation of storybooks or videos about each child is becoming a more feasible teaching practice. This isn't just a cute idea for a special occasion. It's a practical way to create meaningful relationships with families, sharing what we see in their children over the year, responding to their longing to be a part of their children's day and learning process.

Margie Carter

Margie Carter is the co-founder of Harvest Resources Associates (www.ecetrainers.com) and the co-author of numerous books and early childhood videos. As she moves towards retirement years, her professional work is focused on highlighting and supporting the inspiring work of new leaders and uplifting the voices and leadership of teachers in the field.

Goodness of Fit

Matching Families' Expectations for Your Program with Your Own

by Erin Kathleen Kenny

One of the most often overlooked yet critical ingredients for the success of any early childhood program is the support you receive from families. This support arises from the understanding you have with families about the type of program you are running and the match with what they have in mind for their children.

When I first started Cedarsong Nature School's Forest Kindergarten, I was so thrilled that families were signing up for this unique year-round outdoor preschool that I enrolled every family who applied. When families withdrew mid-year because there was a mismatch between our expectations and theirs, I developed a selection process that ensures that each child I enroll is a good match for our specific early childhood education program and that they will continue with our school for the entire year and into the next.

Two families who enrolled in the second year of our program gave me early signs that they would not be able to fully support our program, but I missed these signs. The first child arrived every day in fashionable clothes unsuitable for the weather. While she was eager to be in the forest with us, her mother was less than enthusiastic. Every time it rained, the mother called saying that her daughter was sick or they had an appointment that would not allow her to attend that day. It soon became obvious that the mother was

uncomfortable allowing her child to play out in the rain. This made me wonder why she had enrolled her daughter in our program.

Another child whose family withdrew mid-year also gave me clues I overlooked. In an early class visit, I observed the child dropping his water bottle on the floor and waiting for his mother to bend over and pick it up for him, which she did. This child's father wanted his son to embrace the all-outdoor program we provided, but the mother's ambivalence was apparent: she felt most comfortable doing things for her child. When teachers encouraged him to pick up his own water bottle or challenged him to pick himself up off the ground, he whined and cried for his mother although he was perfectly capable.

The Forest Kindergarten early childhood education model is a novelty in the United States, and prospective families need our assistance in determining if it's the right choice for their children. The Forest Kindergarten program I developed, derived from the German waldkindergartens, is distinguished by a commitment to total nature immersion, interest-led or flow learning and emergent curriculum. Living in a culture, as we do, that promotes early academics for preschoolers, it is vital that prospective parents understand the reasons behind our commitment to the outdoor classroom and why connecting young children to nature is important. We believe that by

Photographs by the author

simply interacting with nature, children are learning valuable natural science principles.

It takes the support of the whole family to make sure the child has the most positive experience possible in our program. I have witnessed situations where either the parent or the child fully embraces our program, but the opposite is not the case. Children may refuse to put their hands in the dirt, or parents don't believe in the nature curriculum we use. The ideal match is with families who appreciate the unique nature of our program and reaffirm our commitment and passion by letting us know that, as one of our first year moms put it, "This school has been a gift to our family in helping our child be confident in himself, close to nature, and true to his own nature."

Early Notification List

Cedarsong accepts applications for admission throughout the school year and maintains an early notification list. This choice, instead of the traditional wait list, does not imply to families that once their turn in line arrives they are automatically enrolled. Every year in April, we hold an open house for all families that submitted applications and were placed on the early notification list. (This event is not otherwise publicized, as we want to ensure that families attending are confident they want to enroll if accepted; in other words, that they know of and embrace our program.) Of course, all currently-enrolled families are invited to secure their space for the following year before I open admissions to new

families. Siblings of currently-enrolled children also have priority for the next year.

Currently-enrolled children and their families are invited to the open house so they may guide prospective new families in understanding more about the commitment they are being asked to make to the program.

Open House and Class-time Visit

After the open house and after all currently-enrolled families have confirmed their spaces for the next year, the teachers and I look over the applications and discuss who we think is a good fit for our program. The families we would like to invite to join our program are required to come for a one-hour class-time visit so we can assess their child's readiness and observe how he or she responds in the group setting. The markers we look for at the class visit are:

■ willingness to immerse in nature.

■ ability to follow teacher directions and rules.

- ability to engage socially with other children.

- ability to leave parent's side while visiting.

- verbal skills in asking for needs to be met.

- positive interactions.

I also require that all children in our program be toilet proficient, as the outdoor setting adds challenges to changing diapers.

During one class-time visit, I observed a little boy who kept running away from the teachers. We had reminded him often that we needed to be able to see him to keep him safe. However, not only did he continue trying to disappear, he would turn to look when we called him and then continue running. I also observed his interactions with his mother that were characterized by whining and clinging behaviors. His mother told me he was not himself that day, having just gotten over being sick. Still, I was concerned. I decided to enroll him for the school year only to withdraw him after the first week when my initial reservations about his challenging behaviors were confirmed.

Teachers' Assessments and Contract

Following the class-time visit, I consult with teachers to make the final decision about whether a family is a good fit for our program. After this final assessment, I send an e-mail to the family either accepting the child into our program or suggesting another preschool program that I think would be a better match.

Creating Community

Creating a community among enrolled families is important to the success of any program. For our families, this means that they have the support of other families who also believe strongly in the principles of our school: that children need a strong and continuing nature immersion experience in order to fully develop to their potential. The parents must be completely on board with their commitment to the all-outdoor model of early childhood education.

When the parents feel connected, they have each other's support for sharing the best ways to make the program work for their family; how to make the transition easier at pick-up and drop off; ideal clothing for outdoor play; and assistance in carpooling. Parents who feel connected to their child's preschool program will be more likely to volunteer to help when needed and are your best source of advertising.

Involving parents in our unique program model has also yielded positive results for families during times when their child is not at school. Many parents have reported that the quality of their outdoor experience has been enhanced by participation in the all-outdoor model. One parent wrote that his son was at a Little League game and, announcing he was hungry, he proceeded to start gnawing on some lichen growing on the side of an alder tree, much to the fascination of his teammates. Another parent reported that her four year old had stopped complaining when they took him hiking and began to engage his parents in a silly nature game he learned at our school.

I encourage parents to make a point of getting their children together outside of class-time so they can forge even stronger connections. This also benefits the social bond that develops between children at school; they learn ways to relate to one another that are not dependent on the school environment. One parent wrote, "Cedarsong is an amazing community of people — it's more than just a school. I have learned so much from the teachers about how to help my kids play cooperatively and creatively and continue to be inspired by the other parents at the school as well." Many parents report that they form strong bonds with other families as a result of their participation in our school.

Creating relationships among the families in our program also ensures that children are given an opportunity to observe peers who respect and appreciate the natural world, and play in it as imaginatively and creatively as they do. The father of one three year old reported that his son had begun exhibiting a gentleness with nature that resulted from his enrollment in our program and that the child had brought the experience back to his city neighborhood by showing care for even the tiniest bugs he uncovered from a rock or the worms he dug up.

Many of our families travel from Seattle and Tacoma and ride the ferry to get to the island where our program is located. Frequently these families schedule an activity together on the island after school, such as a picnic on the beach or at a local playground so parents have a built-in support group. The bonds that are formed strengthen the feeling that their children's school is a special part of their life as a family, and often means they will enroll younger children, too.

We host several events throughout the year that bring all families together:

■ In September, we hold a Family Meet and Greet. Families, children, and siblings are invited to join us at school for a day of play and connection.

■ In December, we hold a Winter Solstice party and Lantern Walk.

■ In February, we have our Parent-Child Nature Play Day.

■ March is the month for our Parents' Night Out.

■ Our end-of-the-year family campout is held in June.

Each of these events is very well-attended and creates warm connections among our families.

Our monthly newsletter for parents highlights what children are learning in our outdoor school. It has become an important way to validate that the children in our program are learning solid natural science principles. It is important that parents be able to articulate the ways in which their children are learning, and the monthly newsletter can give them that ability.

Enrolling families who are a good match for your program is essential to its success. When they witness their child's transformation, parents become some of your strongest champions. Families often report back to me that our program has brought their family closer together through nature exploration time. Children become more comfortable with extended time in nature, so do their parents; the resulting family bond that emerges is invaluable.

Whatever distinguishes your program from others, it is important to consider not only the children you are accepting into your program, but also the parents. You want to make sure that families are a good fit for your program, that you share the same expectations for each other, the program, and the children.

Erin Kathleen Kenny

Erin K. Kenny has been connecting children with nature for over 20 years and is internationally recognized as a leader in the Forest Kindergarten movement. Erin has a Bachelors degree in Environmental Education and a Graduate degree in Environmental Law. Erin co-founded Cedarsong Nature School in 2007 and developed the first U.S. Forest Kindergarten based on the German waldkindergarten early childhood education model. Erin is a passionate and eloquent speaker seeking to inspire and empower others to place priority on nature immersion time for children. Erin created the first U.S. Forest Kindergarten Teacher Training program and has already certified over 40 teachers from all over North America. Cedarsong Nature School recently published Erin's book, *Forest Kindergartens: The Cedarsong Way*, and has produced a documentary DVD *Into the Forest*.

Engaging Families

Contributions of the World Forum Emerging Working Group on Family Engagement

by María Fernanda Levis-Peralta

Children are born and raised in social and economic contexts that have a lasting impact on their lives. Where a child is born, her race, family income, and socio-economic status play important roles in defining the circumstances of her future. Within this context, decades of research demonstrate that parental involvement and family engagement influence children's lives more than any other identified factor. Researchers have even found that "parenting is more important than schools to academic achievement."[1] However, many programs are not fully leveraging the power of engaging families in their work.

Family engagement has been at the core of many important early childhood development programs prompting outstanding results. Yet as all practitioners know, the theory is much neater than the practice. Barriers to involving parents in programs include parent and teacher time, negative attitudes, preconceptions, demographics, employment status, cultural backgrounds, and uncertainty about what to do.[2, 3]

At the 2014 World Forum on Early Care and Education we were able to discuss these issues with scores of practitioners and identified both a growing interest in family engagement and a proliferation of initiatives to reach parents across the globe. The wealth of information provided was extraordinary, and in no way possible to summarize in one article.

However, five strategies used by these programs stand out. Specifically, we found that many of these parental involvement programs are:

- investing resources in strengthening parenting skills.

- engaging parents as change agents in their own communities.

- developing visually stimulating and easy to understand materials.

- using technology to communicate with parents.

- leveraging all the resources at their disposal to partner with parents.

This article provides examples of these strategies across various cultural contexts to be further explored, assimilated, and developed by other practitioners. Our desire is to promote an on-going global exchange of ideas on family engagement to create thriving environments for children and adults.

Five Family Engagement Strategies

■ Investing resources in strengthening parenting skills

A wealth of parenting skill-building programs are available across various cultural contexts. Most of the family engagement programs we encountered are structured as 'stand-alone' programs that provide service to parents not contingent on their engagement in other center-based or formal programs. For example, evidenced-based home visitation programs such as Parents as Teachers, Nurse Family Partnership, and HIPPY have been made available to thousands of parents across the United States through investments in home visitation. In other contexts some of the field's leaders have been using editorials and/or technology to spread their reach at a lower cost. For example, PODAR Education Network in India has added to its system of 72 schools an online platform called BORN SMART to help parents draw on knowledge and resources to help them secure the future of their children; Proud2BMe is addressing the needs of parents in South Africa; and Chiquiespacio.com from Puerto Rico hosts an online platform where parents and experts can exchange information about parenting and projects. Many centers also integrate parenting skills mainly based on their own curriculum; for example, Proyecto Nacer provides skills for teen parents using locally developed materials. More work needs to be done to identify, gather, and share the content and materials used by centers.

■ Engaging parents as change agents in their own communities

We also found that groups are engaging parents as resources for their communities with great success. The work being carried out by Nhaka Foundation in Zimbabwe is a hallmark of this strategy engaging parents in the construction, renovation, and equipment of early childhood development centers, literally having parents building the spaces for their young children. The U.S. Head Start program has also been a pioneer in this area having parents participate in the governance of the center and as volunteers. ParqueREVOLUTION has also begun similar work by engaging parents and community members in the development, construction, and maintenance of parks and play spaces for the entire family as a way of having conversation about what the communi-

ty's aspirations are for its children. Most examples included community-organizing methodologies to involve parents to work towards their community's development. These programs are extremely exciting and inspiring for the transformation they are producing and we are anxious to learn of more examples to highlight.

■ Developing visually stimulating and easy to understand materials

Various family engagement projects also cite visually stimulating and easy to understand materials for parents as key to their success. Editorial Jugando Aprendo publishes educational material for parents in Central America using material that is very attractive and easy to understand; 123kindergarten.com from Canada provides engaging Youtube.com 'to do' videos; and Proud2BMe uses multimedia to engage parents. Our experience at Chiquiespacio.com is that social media engagement is largely based on the quality of the images provided and in our culture what calls the attention most are visuals that highlight children. More research on the type of materials that parents find most engaging can provide insight on how to compete for parent's attention in the sea of information that is being pushed on our families.

■ Using technology to communicate with parents

Technology is increasingly becoming an important tool to reach parents. In addition to the numerous online platforms and websites mentioned in previous sections of this article, Erikson Institute and University of the West Indies have also launched research and practice initiatives to identify and inform with respect to the use of technology for family engagement. This research might reveal different things for different communities in the world. Most of the technology we encountered is being used to provide parents with information to make more informed decisions about their parenting style. Few examples that we encountered were using technology to provide other services to parents and families.

■ Leveraging all the resources at their disposal to partner with parents

What we found is that programs are going to great lengths and investing resources to reach and partner with parents. Some extremely impressive work is being done by parents: for example, in the work presented by Najibullah s/o Tassia from Afghanistan, where parents would literally climb mountains to engage in parenting programs; and Nhaka Foundation, where parents sometimes forego a day of work and food to build spaces for their children to grow and prosper.

Where is the Field of Family Engagement Headed?

Increased importance is being given internationally to family engagement. For example, this past July the U.S. White House and the W.K. Kellogg Foundation (WKKF) held a Symposium on Transformative Family Engagement to examine innovative practices and discuss challenges and opportunities related to these efforts. While a lot is being done, more can be done to identify promising approaches to family engagement across various cultural contexts to inform and support practitioners in these endeavors. Some additional areas where the field can grow include taking into account the cultural appropriateness of interventions, building on the network effects of mobilizing parents, including family engagement skills in ECD teacher training curriculum, using place-based strategies to augment parent participation, and developing technology to support this work.

Family engagement is one of the most underused assets to support children in their development, but we are seeing the spark of a movement to engage parents in helping all children reach their full potential.

Endnotes

1 North Carolina State University. (2012, October 10). Parenting more important than schools to academic achievement, study finds. *ScienceDaily*. Retrieved August 4, 2014 from www.sciencedaily.com/releases/2012/10/121010112540.htm

2 A. Shartrand et al. (1997). *New skills for new schools: Preparing teachers in family involvement*. Harvard Family Research Project. www.hfrp.org/publications-resources/browse-our-publications/new-skills-for-new-schools-preparing-teachers-in-family-involvement

3 Barriers to Family Involvement In Education Kindergarten Teacher Tip #1. http://center.serve.org/tt/ktip1_barriers.pdf

María Fernanda Levis-Peralta

María Fernanda Levis-Peralta is founder of Chiquiespacio.com, Impactivo, Fundación Chana y Samuel Levis, and other social enterprises in the areas of health and education. She is a National Representative for the World Forum Foundation and serves on the Boards of Puerto Rican Minds in Action and Agenda Ciudadana. She is passionate about engaging families and communities to promote health and the well-being of children, helping organizations solve tough problems, and parenting her amazing boy. She is a Robert Wood Johnson Foundation Fellow, holds MPH and MPA degrees from Harvard University, and is a certified Montessori Guide for Infants and Toddlers.

The Family Partnership

by Molly Greenman

So Glad You Asked

As one woman after another described small victories as parents — "I took my son to the playground," "My daughter won the class spelling bee" — Cheryl seemed to disappear into her chair. The group got more and more animated with successive rounds, but Cheryl 'passed' every time. Finally, the other moms insisted there must be something Cheryl did with her kids that she felt good about. "Well, I made a promise to myself I would read to my kids every night, just like my mom did, and I have kept that promise to this day." After a moment of stunned silence, the room exploded: "Every single night?" "Where do you get the books?" "How do you know what books to read?" Cheryl, like many of the other moms present that night, was living in a transitional housing apartment and had been homeless many times over the years. And, like the other moms, she was used to being told what she needed to do to take care of her kids, but not used to being asked what she knew how to do that might benefit others.

In 2000, The Family Partnership was asked by a large local family foundation to come up with a fresh approach to teaching parenting to low-income parents. The result was The Family Project. Its innovation within the field of parent engagement has been to offer alternatives to parenting classes and institutionally-driven parent engagement activities, rethinking

parent involvement in terms of community-building and parent connectedness. It has been particularly successful with low-income families, families of color, and new immigrants, helping to reduce the information and connection gap between parents and the institutions that families interface with — especially schools. Since 2001, more than 15,000 parents and children have been engaged through this work; 84% identified as people of color and 59% as new immigrants. The Family Project has grown into a nationally recognized program, receiving the Annie E. Casey "Family Strengthening Award" from the United Neighborhood Centers of America.

The Family Project model is founded on several assumptions:

- We see parents as the bearers of assets; our job is to help bring those assets to light.

- Change takes place in the context of relationships, and positive change requires mutual trust and respect.

- As people experience being seen, heard, and valued, they begin to believe they have something to offer.

The typical parent we seek to engage is living on a marginal income, uses public transportation, and has limited English language proficiency. Native-born parents usually have their own history of negative school experiences, while immigrants often have very different expectations of their role in their children's education. Finally, isolation is a common thread. These are families that are disconnected from the school community and often their neighborhoods, as well. Particularly, when children are being bused to elementary and pre-schools, the parents are unlikely to know each other.

Most of these parents have heard from the school (and many other professionals in their lives) plenty about what they are not doing, but should do for their children. This is not surprising; we are a nation of problem-solvers, which of course means we have to have problems to solve. And we love experts (think Dear Abby, Judge Judy, Ask This Old House). As educators and social workers, people expect us to have answers, and besides, we put a lot of time, energy, and money into developing our expertise.

We often encounter school personnel, and parent volunteers, who have given up trying to engage the other parents. One principal told me, "I think those parents just don't care!" Class sizes, classroom expectations, and diversity are increasing, while resources, support services, and public confidence are on the wane. It must be really challenging for teachers and school staff to maintain a spirit of equanimity, much less enthusiasm toward parents who don't meet our expectations for involvement.

So, if schools and programs want parents to help their kids to succeed and parents want their children to succeed in school, why do we keep missing the mark? What we have found in The Family Project is that school staff and parents have a hard time listening to each other. School staff experience enormous pressure to share information with parents because of the urgency of educating parents about school choice, meeting No Child Left Behind goals, etc. School staff often think they are listening, when in fact they are doing most of the talking, information sharing, and problem-solving. Parents, for their part, are pretty tired of being talked at, frequently have had negative experiences of their own with school (as both a student AND a parent), and are tired of

coming to school-parent meetings where the entire agenda has been set in advance by the schools.

That's why The Family Project begins by asking questions. When we help parents and schools come together in Family Gatherings, we ask both parties some fundamental questions — usually ones that they have never been asked before. Our first Family Gathering icebreaker question goes quite deep: "What beliefs and values guide you as a parent, or as someone who cares about kids." This question creates an atmosphere of both intimacy AND equality. Practically every time we do this, both parents and school staff say: "We have never been asked this question before."

This conversation sets the stage for other questions:

"What do you think is going on with your child? What do you need to help your kids succeed in school? How can we help?" Sadly again, most of these parents tell us, no one has ever asked them what they thought.

For example, Alejandro's teacher and the school social worker had worked for months to get help for him after he was screened for ADHD. They could not understand why a parent would not follow through on treatment that they had bent over backward to make accessible. They asked our Spanish-speaking school-family liaison to help. She visited the mother and, by asking questions, found out the mom had completely misinterpreted the school's communication. The mom thought ADHD meant she was deficient in paying attention to her son. She was so ashamed, she avoided contact with school officials as much as possible.

We have also learned in our work with parent engagement in schools that immigrant parents are often coming with completely different expectations of schools and themselves. In México, for example, the schools are the authority on a child's education and have the responsibility for the child while in school. Parents are neither expected nor encouraged to get involved and may be seen as meddling if they do.

At the beginning of my comments, I shared Cheryl's story. She persuaded low-income, homeless parents that it is possible to read to their children every night. She answered their questions, which helped them see how they could do this, too. Now if our staff said the same things, those same parents probably would have said: "Get out of here! Stop talking down to us. You have no idea what being homeless is like or how unrealistic you are being about our lives. You're not helping." Even worse, they may not have said but only thought the words, and disengaged from further involvement. But Cheryl showed that everyone can help. Parents can teach each other. Parents have many — perhaps even most — of the answers that other parents need. We just need to create spaces in which they can share what they value, believe, and know with each other. To do that, we have to ask them.

I'm not going to tell you we have all the answers about how to do this. I will offer some questions that you can ask parents, your co-workers, and yourself to begin the conversation:

■ Share a time you felt successful as a parent.

■ What do you think would help your child (get to/ behave better in/do better in) school/child care?

■ What's getting in the way of you helping your child succeed?

■ What was your experience with school/pre-school like? How would you like your child's experience to be the same? Different?

■ What beliefs or values help guide you as a parent? How can we support those in our center?

■ What are some of your family's cultural traditions?

■ What has been your experience with your child's school/center/program?

■ What are your dreams for your child? What are your hopes for your child in this class/program/ center?

■ What's the best way for you to get information about what's going on in this school/class/ program?

■ What does your child like best about you?

■ What support could you use to make sure your child has a good experience in our school/ program?

■ And last, but not least, how can we help your child, your family, and you succeed?!

You may be surprised that staff and parents frequently come up with different answers to the same key questions. For example, when asked what parent engagement means, school staff and child care providers often say:

■ attending conferences.

■ going to PTO meetings.

■ doing what is asked by staff (e.g., filling out forms).

Parents, on the other hand, may say engagement means:

■ "I get my child to the bus every day."

■ "I let the teacher do her job."

■ School staff will greet me when I come into the building, believe what I say about my child, and see my child and me as a source of solutions, rather than problems.

To get you started, it may help to think about what a positive, engaged parent interaction looks like to you:

■ Think of a time when you made a strong, positive connection with a parent.

■ What about that interaction was different than others?

■ What are your strengths as a relationship builder?

■ What might others in your center bring to a parent engagement process?

■ How do you know whether parents think you (and your center) are listening to them and being responsive?

Today, there is a general consensus that early childhood development and learning is essential for children's success in school and life. Most experts agree that parent involvement is key to children's success in school. Early childhood educators can not only jump start young children's learning, you can jump start parent involvement, too.

One more question: What are you waiting for?

Molly Greenman

Molly Greenman, M.S.W., is the President and CEO of The Family Partnership, a 132-year old nonprofit in Minneapolis, Minnesota. Through counseling, education programs, and advocacy, The Family Partnership annually helps more than 20,000 children and families in need and empowers them to solve problems. Ms. Greenman has over 35 years' experience working in direct service and leadership positions.

Moving from Family Participation to Partnerships

Not Always Easy; Always Worth the Effort

by Anne Stonehouse

The early childhood profession has a strong tradition of involving families — that is, finding ways to help families connect with services. Involvement, sometimes called participation, is valuable, but current thinking suggests going beyond involvement to partnerships. It's important to have many ways for families to be involved and participate in the life of the service if they want to; however, family involvement is now seen not as an end in itself, but rather as a means to an end: partnerships with families.

As is true of personal and business partnerships, child care partnerships with families take many forms. The partnership with each family will be unique, but they all have some common characteristics:

- mutual respect

- trust

- sensitivity to the perspective of the other

- ongoing, open, 'both-ways' communication

- common goals that are clear and agreed on: the child's well-being

- clarity about roles and responsibilities

- teamwork; absence of rivalry or competition

- recognition and valuing of the unique contribution and strengths of the partner

- shared decision making.

Respect for families and children is the foundation for healthy partnerships. Children, no matter how young, are active participants in the relationship, and their views are taken into account.

Working in partnership doesn't mean that professionals assume the roles and responsibilities of families — that is, that they take their place. They can't, as families are the most important people in children's lives. Believing that in some ways child care substitutes for family experience and relationships can interfere in a major way with partnerships.

Most child care philosophy and policy statements place importance on good relationships and communication with families. Putting these words and ideas into daily practice is much more challenging than coming up with the words. Many child care professionals would agree that establishing and maintaining partnerships with families is the most complex part of working in child care.

What's the Difference between Family Involvement and Partnerships?

The difference between involvement and partnerships has to do primarily with power and authority. Typically, family involvement consists of families taking up some opportunities offered by professionals to contribute to the operation of the service. These may include such activities as:

■ fundraising.

■ attending working bees.

■ being on committees.

■ contributing materials.

■ organising and/or attending social events, meetings, or talks.

■ helping out with the program.

Most family involvement activities allow the professional to maintain control and power. Genuine partnerships, on the other hand, require professionals to share power. True partnerships mean that families and professionals, along with the child, negotiate the child's experience in child care.

Partnerships require a confident professional who is open to families' priorities and requests and who is clear about areas where compromise or negotiation is not possible. This may be because of regulations, when families' requests do not fit with the service philosophy or policies or are not in the child's best interests. When there are partnerships, families are encouraged to express their concerns, question practices and policies, and ask for what they want. When their requests cannot be agreed to, professionals owe them an explanation, given without any implication that it was inappropriate to ask. Child care professionals need to know what families want for their child in child care and what their concerns are (Greenman, Stonehouse, & Schweikert, 2008). While family participation often focuses on the operation of the service, social events, or parent education, partnership focuses on negotiating the child's experience.

Having a variety of ways for families to become involved is important, and can contribute to a partnership. However, it is possible for families to be very involved and not have a partnership — that is, not have much of a say in their child's experience. Similarly, it is quite possible for families to have robust partnerships with the professionals who care for their child and not be involved in the service.

If Partnerships are Complex and Challenging, Why Bother?

Increasingly, child care services are viewed as not only places for children, but also family support services. This doesn't mean adding program components. It means giving priority to partnerships with families in every area of service operation, but particularly in daily interactions and communication. Working in partnership isn't an extra thing to do, but rather a way of going about everything that you do. It's as much about how you go about your work and the ways you communicate as it is about what you do and say.

Partnerships with Families Lead to Many Benefits for Families, Children, and Professionals

Benefits for professionals:

■ Getting information about the child from an expert on the child

■ Working with a more complete picture of the child, leading to the satisfaction of providing a better experience

■ Greater appreciation by families of professionals' work

■ The satisfaction of knowing that they may be making a lasting positive difference in the life of a child

Benefits for families:

■ Greater confidence about their child's experience

■ Increased confidence in their parenting

■ Belonging to a community of people who care about their child

■ Opportunities to contribute significantly to their child's experience even when they are absent

■ Greater appreciation of their child's uniqueness

■ Additional information about and a different perspective on their child

■ Ongoing reassurance that they are the most special person in their child's life

Most importantly, benefits for the child:

■ The experience of the special people in his or her life working together and with the child, which promotes feelings of security and belonging

■ Consistent, sensitive, individualised experiences

■ Greater continuity between family life and the child care experience

■ Families who feel confident about their child-rearing

■ Relationships in child care that are built on deep knowledge of the child.

As a profession, we now understand much better than we did in the past that in order to support children's learning we need to know them in the context of their family, culture, and community. Ultimately, the reason to strive for mutually respectful partnerships with families is that one of the most important things professionals can do for children is to promote a strong sense of connection and belonging with their family.

What Gets in the Way of Partnerships?

Partnerships aren't easy. Obstacles, in addition to confusion with involvement include:

■ lack of time and staff resources along with competing responsibilities.

■ inclination to 'blame' the other when something goes wrong.

■ narrow view of the role of the child care professional: 'my work is about children, not families'.

■ lack of confidence and skills to work with families.

■ families' expectations — they may not be expecting a partnership.

■ families' lack of confidence — what do I know?

What are Some Practices that Promote Partnerships?

The physical environment. Create a welcoming physical environment that makes a strong statement to families that they belong in child care. Seeing something of their communities, cultures, and lives connects them to the child care and conveys respect.

Informal communication. Prioritise ongoing informal communication. Use a variety of ways, but keep in mind that text messages, e-mails, phone calls, displayed documentation, and exchanged journals are good supplements to brief chats, but they are not a good substitute for them.

'Good news'. Share all the 'good news' you honestly can about their child with families — not just the big events or milestones, but little things as well. This demonstrates to families that you both know and value their child.

'Not so good news'. Think carefully about when and how to share concerns with families. When you do, combine honesty with optimism and professionalism.

Parents as people. Acknowledge in your interactions that parents have many other roles and responsibilities — as workers, partners, or spouses, parents of children other than the one you care for, people with siblings, and parents themselves. In other words, parents are people with complex lives — not just parents!

Empathy. Think about what situations mean from the family's perspective, especially when there are differences or conflicts.

Orientation. Exchange information with families before and at the beginning of a child's participation. Ask them about their child — interests, personal style, routine — and about what they want for their child in the child care setting. Ask them what is important for them about their child's experience. This sets the stage for partnership. Follow up and continue these conversations throughout the child's participation.

Focus. Accept that families will focus more on their own child than the whole group and that families' love for their child means that they cannot be objective about the child. It's your job to be objective.

Encouragement. Encourage families to ask questions, make requests, and engage in constructive criticism. Follow up on these.

Expectations. Just as we do with children, recognize that each family is unique and that families are dynamic. All families have strengths. Some families need considerable ongoing support, and all families need support at times. Individualise expectations for families and avoid stereotyping and making unfounded assumptions.

Fun and joy. Whenever possible, support families in their childrearing and help them to find pleasure in their child. Childrearing can feel like a burden for families — such high expectations, so much professional advice, and so many competing obligations. There are many good ways to rear children and to be a family.

Shared decision making. Involve families whenever you can in making decisions about their child's experience.

Strong connections. Build relationships with other family support services in your community so that you can help families make use of them when they need assistance or information that you cannot provide.

Conflict resolution. Have in place procedures for resolving conflicts and let families know about these. It is inevitable that conflicts will arise around something as important as children's early learning.

In Summary

Partnerships are relationships. Relationships are a matter of heart and mind, a perspective or way of working and not a set of activities or strategies. The focus of the relationship is children's well-being. The main purpose of the relationship is to support children by:

- finding out as much as you can about the children in the context of their family, culture, and communities and using that knowledge to support learning.

- learning from families about the child.

- contributing to families' understanding of their child and appreciation of their child's uniqueness.

- promoting the importance of the family in the child's life.

Just as is the case with personal relationships, partnerships with families are built on many small, often brief, sometimes seemingly insignificant and taken-for-granted encounters — the little things you do and say.

Questions for Reflection

In reflecting on partnerships with families, ask yourself:

■ What is there in the physical environment that says to families "You are welcome here, you belong here"?

■ What messages do families get about their 'place,' their role, in the service — from the communication and the ways professionals go about their work?

■ If you genuinely take on board the message that what matters most in a child's life is the relationship with family and the family's ability to support the child's well-being, how will that affect your work tomorrow? What might you do differently?

References and Resources

Greenman, J., Stonehouse, A., & Schweikert, G. (2008). *Prime times: A handbook for excellence in infant and toddler programs* (2nd edition). St Paul, MN: Redleaf Press.

Stonehouse, A. (2008). *How does it feel? Child care from families' perspectives*. Redmond, WA: Exchange Press.

Anne Stonehouse

Anne Stonehouse has worked as a lecturer, center director, resources developer and provider, and consultant to organizations in the United States and Australia for almost 25 years. She is currently an associate professor of early childhood education at Monash University in Melbourne, Australia.

The ECE Social Worker:

A Vital Piece of Any Family-centered Program

by Kelli Didomenico

"When schools build partnerships with families that respond to their concerns and honor their contributions, they are successful in sustaining connections that are aimed at improving student achievement."

Anne Henderson and Karen Mapp (2002)

In a study conducted by the Southwest Educational Development Lab, A New Wave of Evidence: The Impact of School, Family, and Community Connections on Student Achievement, made the observation in the introductory quote. Studies like this reveal that children who have a strong family support system have a better chance for success in an educational setting.

Quality initiatives, whether at the local, state, or federal level, are all emphasizing family engagement and encouraging programs to do more to bridge the gap between school and home life. How has your Early Childhood Education (ECE) program implemented family engagement? What strategies are you employing to get your busy families to spend more time at your school, engage with other families, and actually listen when you offer support or referrals? This is not an easy thing to accomplish.

Increased family engagement not only improves the child's chances of success, it also greatly improves parenting skills, parental and family resilience, and helps ECE programs connect families with the resources they need. Of course, it makes families feel more connected with the program too, and thereby makes them less likely to leave. It's a win-win for all stakeholders, and, ultimately, investments in family engagement improve quality overall.

ECE programs across the country are serving families with a whole host of pressing needs — without the resources to assist them. Borrowing from the field of social work, holistic services for families (an increasingly popular model of service delivery in ECE) are redefining high-quality services for young children and families. A key component of this model is the social worker employed by ECE programs.

To take action in the lives of families, the ECE program needs to define a true family-centered approach that seeks to provide wraparound care to support not just the child in the classroom, but all family members at home. This family-focused model allows the organization to increase student retention, provide important services, and build bridges in the community to help every family succeed.

The Case for Increasing Overhead

We live in a world where cost cutting and expense watching are championed; where using words like *downsize* or *cut back* is rewarded; where cutthroat management gurus are reality television heroes. Obviously expense management is essential to the longevity and success of any operation (for-profit or non-profit). However, there is a clear limit to how lean you can get, especially in an organization that exists to provide high-quality services for our youngest children and their families.

All ECE programs that have been able to weather the recent economic downturn have had to make some difficult decisions and get creative with cost-cutting measures. These decisions have been vital. Yet the smart program owner or manager knows that there is one area where ECE programs should always invest: family engagement.

ECE program leaders need to recognize the growing need for family support and resources. To fill this need, successful ECE programs may consider creating a special position in the company for a social worker. This is a role that is not required, not common in the industry, and not cheap; but it is necessary. Families need the support of someone who will take their calls directly, answer questions, reply to their comments and address their concerns. This person also can train and support program staff in forging relationships with families and community partners, partnering with them to provide the services that struggling families so urgently need. Hiring a social worker shifts the business model of the ECE program to focus on family, community connections, and a therapeutic approach to child care.

A social worker can build partnerships with community agencies to provide better services for families. For example, at The Children's Workshop one such partnership is with an agency called Kids Connect. Kids Connect is an inclusive therapeutic child care program that helps children with special needs to be successful in mainstream child care settings. The collaboration allows families of children with special needs to choose a local child care facility instead of traveling long distances for a special program. Often, when centers are unable to meet the needs of children with learning disabilities or behavioral issues, the child is suspended and bounced to a different program. Advocating for these families and forging a relationship with an agency like Kids Connect may allow a child to stay in the ECE center of choice and interact with mainstream children within a stable environment in the community.

There are many other ways that cash-strapped programs could benefit from the services of a social worker. A social worker can make arrangements with local nonprofits or community partners to exchange services. For example, a local high school offers parenting classes for pregnant teens and they need a space to meet. A local ECE program has an infant classroom equipped with cribs, high chairs, safe play areas, and baby supplies. The ECE program allows the high school to host classes at the center after hours. In return, the high school sends students with an interest in the field of early education to volunteer at the center as unpaid interns.

Many colleges and universities require students to complete an internship in their field as part of their education. A social worker can connect with college students in many fields including Early Education, Social Work, Psychology, Pediatrics, and Nursing to volunteer at the center. These internships can help an ECE program without increasing payroll costs. Practicing students can also bring new ideas and techniques from the classroom into the field, potentially improving the ECE program's overall curriculum and enhancing the uniqueness of the program. These students eventually graduate and become ideal candidates for the ECE program with a preexisting understanding of how the center operates.

A Family-focused Business Model

How does a family-focused business model work? Hiring someone with a background in social work equips your ECE program with a focused staff member who has already prepared for emergencies that many parents are ill-equipped to handle. For example, imagine that one night a single working mother picks up her children at your center and returns to her apartment to find her locks were changed. Her landlord ran into some legal troubles, and as a result the state seized the property where she was living. With no relatives or friends in town, she may not know where to turn. If her program has a family-focused model in place, the staff at the center can call the social worker and offer immediate assistance. An experienced social worker would know how to find emergency housing for the family and would have established partnerships with community agencies that can provide the distressed parent with legal help. The program can collect food and clothing for the family from other families at the ECE program to help as they try to get back on their feet. These actions foster a sense of community within the program and instill loyalty in the family that they helped and those who witness it.

In addition to strengthening the families at the ECE program, the social worker can also train teachers and other staff members on how to deal with such difficult situations. With a background in guidance, counseling, and support, a social worker can:

■ show teachers how to communicate with and assist a vulnerable parent.

■ support teachers when they need to have difficult conversations about a child's behavior or development.

■ act as an unbiased third party if arguments ensue.

■ advocate for teachers who need to make calls to Child Protective Services about a child's condition or situation, assisting them through the process and advising them on how to respond to questioning.

■ provide a new perspective on a situation through the lens of their experiences.

Furthermore, a social worker can assist teachers in furthering their education. He or she can develop relationships with local colleges and universities to help employees earn certifications and degrees to move forward in their field as professionals. A social worker can set up cohorts with educational institutions and assist in finding grants and scholarships.

For children with behavioral issues, a social worker can build bridges with community resources to provide support. For example, perhaps an ECE program has a family that has a particularly difficult behavioral problem erupting at home. The social worker can refer the family to a program where the parent and child can be supported in developing an Individualized Education Plan (IEP). Having previous knowledge of the system, a social worker can coach the family, giving them the confidence they need to advocate for their child and take control of the process. With the results of the IEP, the social worker can assist the family in finding the proper placement for the child and even go so far as to provide wraparound care and supervision for the child at the ECE program for the rest of the day, if appropriate. Knowledge of the administration and connections with community members will help the family get through a difficult situation, ultimately resulting in a healthier environment for the child.

Community involvement can make a world of difference to a family facing insurmountable obstacles. The role of a child care center and its connections to the community are vital in the life of a family. An ECE company that shifts its business model to focus not only on the child in the classroom, but also the family foundations at home, will add immeasurable quality and benefits to the program. Building bridges in the community allows the ECE provider to offer services beyond child care, retain children in school longer, and build stability in family life at home. These practices help retain customers and ultimately strengthen the bottom line. More importantly, they fulfill our shared mission to nurture children, support families, and build communities.

Reference

Henderson, A. T., & Mapp, K. L. (2002). *A new wave of evidence: The impact of school, family, and community connections on student achievement.* Austin, TX: The National Center for Family and Community Connections with Schools.

Kelli Didomenico

Kelli Didomenico brings over 20 years of experience to her role as Director of Family Engagement at The Children's Workshop. In her role she welcomes and supports children and families directly and supports the company's center directors in encouraging families to become actively involved in their child's education through parent committees, family events, and by volunteering in the classroom. Additionally, she reaches out to form partnerships that enhance the services that The Children's Workshop can provide for its families. Kelli earned her bachelor's degree in Social Work from Rhode Island College.

Lean on Me

Helping Children and Families through Disruptive Change

by Jane Humphries and Kari Rains

Many programs are dealing with change in the lives of the young children in their care. This change is disruptive to a child's emotional competence and can create stress for early childhood program directors and teachers. What is most important for programs to recognize is that these children are experiencing major disruptions in their care by the primary adults outside of the early childhood program. Children are often caught in the chaos of changing living situations, caregiver entry into or exit from their lives, and financial strain. This article focuses on change in the lives of three children in one early childhood program.

Initially, the program director and teachers realized that the consistent and caring early childhood program offered the most stable environment in these children's lives. The flood of emotions displayed by each child required a sensitive and knowledgeable adult within the classroom to provide support for healthy social and emotional expression.

Communication with each one of the families was paramount. While sometimes difficult and uncomfortable, beginning conversations with the focus on the child was this director's strategy. Both the director and teachers viewed their roles as collaborative. When advocating for the children, each made a commitment to lend support to each other as well as to the children in their care. After these foundational talks, the director turned her attention to the three-year-old classroom where twins were struggling with their parents' divorce.

Taylor and Tate began acting out during routine activities in the classroom. Drop-off, pick-up, and circle times were occasions for extreme negative behavior: biting and difficulty participating in activities. At mealtimes they grabbed other children's food, pushed chairs over, and yelled. To complicate matters, the teachers in the classroom felt caught in the middle of the twins' parents. The situation was becoming too much for the staff to deal with, and other parents were beginning to complain about the twins' behaviors.

At times like this the director's professional influence and role is key. Initial steps included the director calling each parent separately to acknowledge the difficulty the teachers were having with communication, as well as the children's emotional outbursts. The director communicated to both parents that a meeting —either together or separate —was crucial for addressing the needs of the children. By keeping the focus on the children's needs, the director was able to schedule both parents for the same meeting place and time. Care for the children was arranged and provided by a teacher assistant. The meeting agenda was set to include establishing expectations for communication and boundaries between the parents and with staff, as well as sharing strategies to help the twins manage their strong emotions.

On the day of the meeting, Tate and Taylor's parents met with their teacher and the director; it was agreed that:

■ a spiral-bound journal would be kept in the classroom to foster communication between the parents and all involved in the care of the children.

■ the director would put all financial information related to the children's account in two separate envelopes; that way everyone had equal access to information and this limited the tense communications felt by the teachers and director.

■ a picture schedule placed in each child's cubby along with a photo book with pictures of their mom, dad, and other family members would help facilitate the twins' movement between the parents' homes. The picture schedule showed the classroom routine and activities as well as the routine at home. The parents would add or change pictures of where the twins would be in the evening and what they would be doing. These visual cues helped clarify expectations for the twins.

■ the children would be given special assistance during difficult times: circle time, transition, and nap.

• Each would be given small items such as a squishy ball, Busy Hands™ (see Resources), or other objects during times of upset or distress to help calm and facilitate emotional regulation. The items were small enough for the children to carry with them and use when they felt overwhelmed or were seeking out sensory stimulation. The objects also helped when the group needed to transition. The teachers noticed that when Tate had access to items with different textures he rubbed these against his face, which helped him calm and regulate his emotions during nap time. The director and teachers allowed Taylor and Tate to take their items home with them. Over time it was found to be a great transitional object and support that helped with consistency in addressing behavior across all environments.

• Naptime for Tate included moving him to a more open space in the classroom away from other children and allowing him to manipulate his small object until he drifted off to sleep.

■ to combat his angry yelling, Tate would be encouraged to yell into the "Mad Jar" that his teachers made, with his help. The jar was placed in his cubby and could be easily accessed when he needed to 'get his mad out.' After a couple of times being coached on how to use the "Mad Jar" by his teachers, Tate took full advantage of the strategy. Initially he used it a lot, but over time his use tapered off as he began to regulate his emotions on his own.

■ the parents would implement a "Mad Jar" at both parents' homes when they learned of its effectiveness.

With multiple approaches and strategies in place to assist the twins, the director could turn her attention to an issue in the toddler room with a child who had been at the program for a little over a week.

While Rashaun seemed to accept the initial enrollment and participation in the early childhood program, within days he began clinging to his aunt at drop-off and crying if he was not held by his teacher throughout the day. The teachers in his classroom, while trying to help Rashaun manage his feelings, were struggling to manage their responsibilities for the classroom. Rashaun required so much attention. Due to the delicacy of this child's situation, the director and teachers wanted to understand more about attachment and trauma, to communicate regularly with his aunt, and to think of ways to provide consistency in his day to help cope with his emotions.

At 18 months of age, Rashaun's opportunity to live with his aunt came as a major life change. Fortunately, Rashaun's aunt had been involved in his life from a very early age. When the director and teachers observed Rashaun closely in the first few days of his enrollment, he talked about his aunt "Mama" and happily greeted her each day when she picked him up. As the director and teachers began developing a relationship with his aunt, they learned that Rashaun's mother had made an abrupt and traumatic departure from his life. This included the police coming to their home in the night only a few weeks earlier and taking her away in handcuffs by the police, and his being taken into protective custody. The next morning his aunt, who was contacted by child protective services, assumed custody. Within days, she had located the program and enrolled him, as she needed to return to work herself.

Children in this age group are still developing attachments to caregivers. Attachments can be nurtured during this developmental age by consistent responses to distress, reliable caregivers, and positive peer interactions. For Rashaun, attachment to significant adults had been difficult as a result of the trauma in his life.

In initial conversations, the director and Rashaun's aunt decided:

■ his aunt would stay for a few more minutes at drop-off until he was engaged in activity and transferred into the care of a teacher. This included having Rashaun's aunt bring him to the program at a designated time every morning so that extra staff were on hand to help.

■ extra staff would allow Rashaun's teachers to focus on him, by holding him and then helping engage him in a classroom activity. As research has found, touch is essential for children's growth, development, and overall health, as well as the primary means to foster healthy child-caregiver attachment.

■ his aunt would bring a picture of him with his aunt and a special object from home (e.g. stuffed bear, blanket) to school. When he longed for her, he could pull out the picture as well as the special toy to allow him to remember his special relationship with his aunt and to be close to something that was special to him throughout the day.

■ the teachers would have Rashaun sit in their laps during group times and make efforts to engage him in leadership roles with classroom duties, such as carrying toys for them.

Within a few days, the classroom began to run more smoothly. A coordinated and consistent routine began to emerge. While it was a bumpy first few days, Rashaun recognized the daily routine and he began to initiate his own play and engaged in class activities with his peers. Rashaun's aunt remained consistent with the time she dropped him off and reported that the schedule had helped to settle him down at home. The director and teachers found that while the initial investment of time was great, within a few weeks Rashaun's transition into the program was complete.

When it came time to facilitate his movement into the next classroom, Rashaun was slowly introduced and spent one-on-one time with his new teachers over the course of a month. His aunt was also involved in this transition, visiting the new classroom at drop-off and pick-up while Rashaun was with her. She also talked about his new teachers and friends when she and Rashaun were at home. Overall, the collaborative effort helped Rashaun through a very difficult time in his life. Developing secure and safe attachments at this age was crucial to his developing a sense of trust; and it was imperative that the early childhood program provide, in conjunction with his aunt, as much consistency in caregiving and routine as possible.

The children described here needed caring support from their teachers and the director. A key element was the communication between the significant adults in these children's lives. In addition, consistent nurturing responses to behavior in the classroom helped ease the children's adjustment and activities were carefully planned to address their needs. Ultimately, the staff within this early childhood program accepted these challenging situations with a high degree of professionalism and commitment to the families and children involved. This included ongoing access to information to increase their personal knowledge and understanding. Their commitment to each child's ability to adjust and build their emotional competence was met with an informed, coordinated, calm, and nurturing environment — ALL essential ingredients when dealing with significant change in the lives of children.

Resources

Bruce, N., & Cairone, K. (2011). *Socially strong, emotionally secure: 50 activities to promote resilience in young children.* Lewisville, NC: Gryphon House.

Hewitt, D. (2012). *So this is normal too?* (2nd edition). St. Paul, MN: Redleaf Press.

Kaiser, B., & Rasminsky, J. (2012). *Challenging behavior in young children understanding, preventing, and responding effectively* (3rd edition). Upper Saddle River, NJ: Pearson.

Saifer, S. (2003). *The early childhood teacher's manual: Practical solutions to practically every problem.* St. Paul, MN: Redleaf Press.

Sperry, R. (2011). *FLIP-IT: Transforming Challenging Behavior.* Devereux Center for Resilient Children. Retrieved from www.devereux.org/site/PageServer?pagename=az_resilient_children_2015

"Busy Hands"™ can be found at www.fiddlefocus.com, a product of Creative Educational Strategies & Services LLC.

Jane Humphries and Kari Rains

Jane Humphries and Kari Rains are with an Oklahoma-based company called Creative Educational Strategies & Services. They are dedicated to providing educators, administrators, parents, and other caregivers with the information and research that supports best practices when working with children and adults, especially those who struggle in the areas of social and emotional development. To read more about their innovative products, ideas and services go to www.fiddlefocus.com.

the Art of
LEADERSHIP

ENGAGING FAMILIES
IN EARLY CHILDHOOD ORGANIZATIONS

2
CHAPTER 2
Communicating with Parents

The Ten Ps of Parent Communication

by Timothy Wayne Borruel

There are many ingredients that contribute to a successful preschool — dedicated staff, safe environment, and programs to help children with socialization and early academic skills. And high on this list is communication — specifically staff-parent communication. Through regular communication with parents, staff members help develop, nurture, and maintain relationships that, in turn, lead to parent confidence in the preschool program. When parents develop an open and close relationship with their child's teacher, even mistakes and errors are easily forgiven.

It is important to stress that these relationships don't just happen. Instead, they are built. In fact, a quality preschool will require that each and every representative of the school work hard at establishing and maintaining strong parental relationships. All staff should be trained and held accountable for consistently investing in relationships and continually displaying a *service mentality* — which means always showing respect and appreciation to the customer — i.e., parents.

The goal of the *Ten Ps of Parent Communication* is to make parents feel special and cared for — each and every day. This customer service is found in the most well-respected organizations in the country, from Disneyland to Nordstrom's to the Ritz Carlton Hotels. A preschool center that practices the *Ten Ps of Parent Communication* — fostering meaningful relationships with parents — will be well on its way to becoming a respected and quality program.

1 — Professionalism

A teacher's dress and general appearance is paramount in making an initial and lasting impression on a parent. If teachers want to be respected as professionals, they must look and act like professionals — meaning that baggy sweats, dingy t-shirts, and ragged jeans should never be worn in the school. Although office dress may not be the most conducive for working with children, dressing up rather than down will communicate respect for the position. This holds true for grooming and hygiene, which should be impeccable. A teacher's language and mannerisms also communicate either maturity and good judgment or immaturity and instability. Addressing parents with respectful titles like Mr., Mrs., or Dr. communicates respect — in sharp contrast to "dude" and "hey, man." An orderly and organized classroom also communicates professionalism. It shows a desire to be a teacher of excellence and a professional who cares about the job he or she is doing. Of course, a professional teacher also does the following:

■ Returns calls within 24 hours.

■ Proofs all correspondence that goes out from the school, assuring no spelling errors.

■ Avoids discussing confidential issues with peers or other parents.

■ Handles phone conversations with courtesy, politeness, and closure.

2 — Parent Relationship Development

Relationships with parents must be initiated and made a priority. Parents should be greeted every day with a smile, a warm hello, and a question. A teacher should stand right at her door for drop-off and exude enthusiasm and excitement for the day ahead. She should also ask questions such as: "How was your weekend?"; "Did the soccer game go well?"; "How was Heather's birthday party?" At pick-up time, the same kinds of questions should be asked of parents.

What does this do? One simple, yet profound thing — it tells parents that teachers are interested in them. Learning parents' names quickly also demonstrates that the teacher has an interest in developing a relationship. Learning parents' names may seem like a challenge.

In fact, we have all been introduced to someone and literally two seconds later his or her name is gone from our memory and we are forced to ask, "What was your name again?" However, there is one simple suggestion that really works. When teachers first meet parents and learn their names, they should use the name several times in the statements they make during the next several minutes. When a name is used over and over again during an initial conversation, the brain will record it and remember it. If the name isn't used, it is lost. At Sunshine Child Care and Learning Center there is a "Ten Foot Rule." Anyone who comes within ten feet of a staff member must receive three things: 1) a warm greeting; 2) a smile and a question; and 3) a fond farewell.

3 — Positive

A teacher must be positive about one very special person — the child. Each teacher must work hard at being an encourager, a child's biggest fan. Teachers should always have something nice to say about the child, and this should be clearly stated with enthusiasm in front of both the child and the parent. Complimenting parents on their job of parenting is another way to be positive. Parents are working at raising a morally responsible child. So when they are producing fruits from their labor, let them know about it.

Teachers should also be positive about what is happening in their classroom. This can be accomplished by developing a surprise pin or note reward to present to a child at pick-up. This is especially effective with a difficult child. Parents also appreciate a complimentary note home or a quick phone call (60 seconds or less) just to hear that their child is appreciated and doing great.

4 — Personable

Teachers must do their best every day to be friendly — even when they don't feel like it. Individuals who are 'other oriented' and not focused on themselves will be known as friendly and kind persons. Staff members should also remember to smile — it is the universal language of friendliness.

5 — Proactive

Staff should not wait for a parent to initiate conversation. Instead, they should speak first, inquiring about the parent's day or commenting on the great time the child had. When asked how a child's day was, teachers should avoid just saying "fine" and instead be prepared with some adjectives or experience to give the parents a clear picture of the day's events.

Teachers should also offer to genuinely serve the parents. This could be as simple as helping them gather up their child's belongings to expedite pick-up, or it could mean having their child ready to go, knowing that this is a rush evening for the family.

Finally, constantly and consistently use the Ten Foot Rule. Give each parent each day: 1) a warm greeting; 2) a smile and a question; and 3) a fond farewell — and remember to use his or her name.

6 — Passion About Being a Teacher

Teachers should openly display and verbalize their desire to impact a child's life in a positive way. Remembering that a teacher is responsible for creating the next generation is fuel to stay motivated.

Teachers should let parents know that they love what they do and that they wouldn't have it any other way. Parents should also know that the teacher is serious about wanting to make a difference in the life of their child.

7 — Problems: Communicated Tactfully and Skillfully

Teachers should always respect parents' confidentiality by pulling them to the side or behind a closed door when reporting a problem. It is extremely helpful to always start out with a positive statement about the child before informing the parents of a problem or behavior.

To illustrate, try not to say something like, "Kayla was extremely defiant today." This communicates to a parent that "you are really doing a lousy job of parenting." Rather, say, "Kayla continues to be a very sweet girl in my class. However, during circle time today she had some difficulty cooperating with our rules."

Instead of appearing like a tattletale, it is helpful to say to a parent, "We feel you should know what is

happening in the class during the day, so you can respond appropriately at home."

8 — Present the Day's Happenings

Parents need to know the activities of the day so they can engage in conversation with their child. Informing them of the activities and highlights on a dry erase board by the door or on an easel prop allows them the opportunity to read about the day before they even see their child.

Through this strategy, when parents say to their child, "What did you do today?" and the child responds with the traditional "nothing," the parent can ask, "Well, what about Sammy the snake? I heard he was in your class today." On the dry erase board, make the day sound fun and exciting — and make it colorful.

9 — Philosophy Upheld

Every preschool should have a philosophy — one that is upheld by the staff. The Sunshine philosophy stresses three components of learning: socialization, academics, and character.

- **Socialization** — The classroom is an ideal environment for children to learn how to cooperate and share with their peers. Whether it is learning to cooperatively build a house with wooden blocks or playing imaginative games on the playground, children are encouraged to work together in a positive and considerate way.

- **Academics** — Children are gradually taught simple academic concepts such as shapes and colors, and then move to numbers, alphabet letters and sounds, and writing their very own names.

- **Character** — Character is built into the very fabric of the curriculum. Children are encouraged to be respectful, kind, polite, honest, and fair. When they display these traits, they receive mountains of praise.

This philosophy is upheld by every teacher at Sunshine. Preschool teachers should learn their center's philosophy and uphold it. This will send a consistent message to children and their parents each and every day.

10 — Parent Assessment

Once per month, an anonymous parent or colleague should walk through the preschool center and evaluate the kind of communication and service he or she receives from staff. This should be a starting point for evaluating the center's effort to enhance staff-parent communication.

It's important to note that the *Ten Ps of Parent Communication* is not a one-time event, but rather an on-going strategy that should be followed day in and day out. Creating an early childhood center of excellence takes a great deal of effort and focus, but it is certainly worth the investment — both in terms of parent satisfaction and experiencing high enrollment levels. A good reputation is worth more than fine gold.

Being service-minded and other-oriented can help transform a school from average to excellent and create a reputation for responsiveness and quality — a reputation that is priceless in today's educational environment.

Timothy Wayne Borruel

Tim W. Borruel, MA, is the founder and executive director of Sunshine Child Care & Learning Centers and Legacy Private Academy, which together care for and educate 1,500 children a day in six locations throughout the Santa Clarita Valley — about 30 miles north of downtown Los Angeles. He supervises a staff of approximately 175 employees. For the past 17 years, Mr. Borruel has developed and directed the growth and expansion of Sunshine's preschool, school-age, summer camp, and private school programs. Legacy Private Academy's new building, scheduled for completion in 2002, will eventually provide educational services for children through the eighth grade.

Communicating with Parents

by Margie Carter

Everywhere I go I see early childhood programs struggling to find a more effective means of communication with and involvement of parents in their programs. Though everyone believes this is a critical component of quality, hardly anyone is satisfied with what is happening. There is a longing for something more, something different. The longing we feel is about some deeper issues in our lives — lack of time, lack of extended family and community. Instead we have tight schedules, traffic congestion, the stresses of single and shared parenting, low wages, precarious health, and financial instability plaguing both the workers and families in our child care programs.

It seems like staff and families could be a mutual support system for each other; but instead, they typically have complaints and irritations with each other. There is a genuine dissatisfaction with the level of communication between them. To be sure, there are exceptions to this state of affairs, but that's what they are: exceptions. Caregivers long for the kind of respect, support, and community involvement they hear their Italian counterparts have in the schools of Reggio Emilia. Most families in the U.S. don't know about Reggio, but they have their own ideas of what they want from their child's program, their worries about school readiness, and the pressures placed on their family life. They find they just can't take the time to read a notice, help with a field trip, or attend a meeting. Child care staff and parents are each unsettled by the expectations they have of each other. In many settings I hear things like:

Parent: "When I ask Robert what he did in school, he says he just played. Aren't you teaching him anything?"

Teacher: "When we had our parent meeting, only four people showed up. Don't these parents even care about what their children are doing?"

Director: "I spend hours every month putting together a parent newsletter to keep families informed. Judging from the questions and comments I get on any given day, I don't really think anyone reads our newsletter."

At the heart of these mutual frustrations is genuine desire to know what's happening on the other end, along with the parent and caregiver's need to be understood, appreciated, and respected. Is there a way to get beyond the disappointments and gripes and create the kind of communication we all long for?

Strategy:
Introduce Parents to a New Quality of Knowing

The programs I see with better success in parent involvement and communications have gone beyond the typical gimmicks or generic ideas we typically read about. Instead, they have created a tangible way for parents to see their children and the life of the program where they spend oh-so-many hours.

With an active practice of creating individual children's portfolios and documentation displays charting evolving understandings, skills, and curriculum projects, there is a smoother flow of communication and a growing sense of community among parents.

In writing about what is needed to make an alliance between schools and families succeed, Loris Malaguzzi says,

"Teachers must leave behind an isolated mode of working that leaves no traces. Instead, they must discover ways to communicate and document the children's evolving experiences at school. They must prepare a steady flow of quality information targeted to parents but appreciated also by children and teachers. This flow of documentation, we believe, introduces parents to a quality of knowing that tangibly changes their expectations.

"With regard to the children, the flow of documentation creates a second, and equally pleasing, scenario. They become even more curious, interested, and confident as they contemplate the meaning of what they have achieved. They learn that their parents feel at home in the school, at ease with the teachers,

and informed about what has happened and is about to happen."

The Hundred Languages of Children (Norwood, NJ: Ablex Press, 1993)

The idea of "introducing parents to a quality of knowing that tangibly changes their expectations" is a powerful one and not something that can happen overnight. First, the caregivers and teachers have to have that quality of knowing. Documentation displays contribute a great deal to that quality of knowing. Then, teachers must develop skills to articulate what they understand, translating their professional knowledge into user-friendly language.

For the *quality of knowing* to deepen for both teachers and parents, we have to move away from superficial reports about lunch, birthdays, and crafts projects in our communication to parents. These are akin to idle chatter when it comes to the real meaning of what might be happening in our programs. Observant teachers building on children's interests, experiences, and relationships in their curriculum planning have a wealth of significant classroom events to re-represent to both the children and their families. The sense of history and community that grows from this shared documentation is the stuff dreams are made of. It has little to do with the small boxes in a typical lesson plan or a write-up that is posted for parents. Master teacher Ann Pelo describes her beginning work with documentation this way:

"Picking up on the children's interest in the wheelchair accessible sign we noticed on our neighborhood walk, I returned to sketch a curriculum web with 'wheelchair accessibility/ramp building' in the center. This was not intended to be the curriculum plan for the month, but rather a guidepost for traveling with emergent curriculum. I also wanted to begin a record of our project, our classroom history as it developed.

"In the weeks that followed, I took many photos, made and kept copies of the children's letters and drawings, and transcribed tape-recorded conversations among the children. These were displayed for parents as a map of our growing curriculum . . . the children used the documentation as a common frame of reference and would often take out the 'Ramp Book' (a display album) and tell each other the stories of the photos and letters in it."

Strategy:

Parents Introduce Themselves with Documentation Displays

During this past year I've heard several wonderful examples of programs getting parents involved in creating documentation displays about some aspect of their family life. At the Enrichment Center in Research Triangle Park, North Carolina, parents were given a list of possible ways to create displays about their families to post during the Week of the Young Child. Most used photos as part of their display, incorporating varying forms such as mobiles, poems, stories, and family trees.

Carolyn Edwards at the University of Kentucky described a documentation project, which involved creating family history displays.

Wrestling with what to do about diverse and divisive perspectives on holiday practices among the families at their center, the staff at Kidspace Child Care in Seattle, Washington, invited each family to take home an empty display board to fill it up with representations of their favorite winter holiday practices. As these were returned for display in the center, families and staff discovered common values as well as unique ways of celebrating.

Strategy:

Create Dialogue in Newsletters, on Bulletin Boards

Rather than limit our precious bulletin board space and routine newsletters to announcements and fluffy news, why not turn them into avenues of dialogue between parents and staff? Try gathering input from different folks on topics such as "childhood is a time of . . . ," "what school-readiness means to me," "my

favorite childhood summer memory," perhaps using these write-ups with related photos or illustrations. If our child care programs provide ways for parents and staff to get to know each other better, relationships of mutual interest and respect grow. This is in contrast to a bulletin board or child's cubby packed with notices that no one has an interest in reading.

Strategy:

Post Questions Rather than Reports

Parents are often frustrated when they can't get much information from their children about what went on during the day. Teachers find they don't have time to write much more than a quick summary of what went on and, more often than not, this summary isn't of great significance to parents.

To help parents apply what we know about building verbal expression in children, try posting an open-ended question, rather than a report, on the classroom door at the end of the day. For instance, if you had a pet snake visit the classroom, suggest to parents: "Ask your children what animals they think make good pets." Or, if you are doing a curriculum project around water, suggest that parents raise a question about where water comes from or goes when they are washing dishes or getting ready for a bath.

Helping parents learn the value of using descriptive language and open-ended questions will assist them in soliciting stories from their children. This, in turn, will encourage parents to stay in closer contact with caregivers and teachers because they value help and expertise.

Strategy:

Spread the News of Successful Partnerships

There are always parents who go out of their way to build a relationship with their child's caregivers, who eagerly seek out advice and work closely to maintain consistency between home and their child care center. As you recognize this happening, ask if you can share this story with others. Broadcasting these examples of how a good partnership works (via your newsletter, bulletin boards, or other visual displays) will capture the attention of other families in your program and enhance their interest in forming a closer care-giving partnership.

Margie Carter

Margie Carter is the co-founder of Harvest Resources Associates (www.ecetrainers.com) and the co-author of numerous books and early childhood videos. As she moves towards retirement years, her professional work is focused on highlighting and supporting the inspiring work of new leaders and uplifting the voices and leadership of teachers in the field.

Using the Principles of Intentional Teaching to Communicate Effectively with Parents

by Jody Martin

Acting 'intentionally' means acting purposefully with a carefully considered goal in mind. We know that the intentional teacher:

■ creates clearly-defined learning objectives when planning a lesson for her children.

■ assesses their progress and modifies activities as needed. (Epstein, 2007)

■ develops clear communication objectives regarding her program, child development in general, and the child's progress.

■ provides this information in such a way that parents can understand and access it easily.

■ assesses periodically whether the communication system or materials are effectively being used by the parents and modify, if needed.

When families and teachers work as a team and communicate freely, it can provide benefits for everyone in the program. A teacher will feel more effective and confident if the relationship with families involves two-way communication and is one of mutual respect and support. Families benefit because they can feel secure and confident when they leave their children with the teacher. This two-way communication creates a solid partnership that provides essential information to both parents and teachers.

Another important factor in two-way communication is addressing parent concerns. Ann Epstein (2007) advises:

"Parental concerns should never be dismissed, nor should they be seen as the 'enemy' of appropriate practice. Rather, they should be respected, and teachers should emphasize the commonalities between home and school goals for children's education" (p. 20).

Teacher-guided versus Parent-initiated Communication

An effective early childhood program combines child-guided and adult-guided educational experiences (Epstein, 2007). In much the same way, an effective atmosphere of communication exists when there is a combination of teacher-guided and parent-initiated communication, where teacher and parent have active roles in the communication process. The teacher plays an integral role in the parent-initiated communication and the parent has a significant, active role in the teacher-guided communication.

Intentional teachers understand that both modes of communication are valid and that offering both to parents will allow them to choose what works best for them with their schedule and style of communicating. For example, parents who have three children in a school for several years may actually need less communication because they have a good rapport with the teachers and management and trust that their children had a good day:

■ They have gained lots of knowledge over the years and know the quality and consistency of the school.

■ Their children may be older and can share about their own day.

■ By their own choice, they need less communication.

■ They would then be using less of the parent-initiated technique of communication.

■ They would rely on basic daily communication that the teacher provides.

There will always be those new parents who have never experienced leaving their child in someone else's care and will need a great deal of communication initially.

■ These parents will want to absorb everything they can about child development and will want to know every detail of their child's day.

■ They will definitely use the parent-guided means of communication until they are comfortable. Then will rely more on the information the teacher offers each day.

It's being able to read the communication style and expectations of each parent that is being 'intentional' about communicating.

Having said this, it is still very important to let all parents know about the various means of communication that are available. Some communication pieces will be obvious in the classroom environment and some will need to be explained. Encourage parents to take advantage of all the resources that are provided and to participate in any interactive communication vehicles that exist. Be sure to give positive reinforcement when a parent uses resources. Survey parents and ask for feedback to help you focus on specific communication techniques or tools that are most effective.

Helping Parents to Become More Intentional with Their Children

In her article, "Mapping Family Resources and Support," Tess Bennett (2007) says, "The teacher is an early childhood professional who is intimately involved with the family on behalf of the child." We know that the relationship a teacher develops with a family can have a powerful effect on the child's learning. The learning can be further enhanced if teachers help parents to become more intentional in their interactions with their children. You can do this by:

■ educating parents on child development through articles and e-mail links so that they can learn more about their child's age-specific development, the latest brain research findings, and parenting issues. A good example of this is the Body, Mind and Child website: www.bodymindandchild.com, which hosts interviews with early childhood education experts.

■ giving them activity ideas to extend the learning at home. Provide handouts of activities, songs, and finger plays that relate to your theme or the skills and concepts the child is working on.

■ providing information regarding the developmental level and progress of their child. You can do this through daily and weekly notes and monthly progress checklists that relate to the theme and concepts being taught. Ultimately you will be providing them with the tools to be more intentional in their interactions with their children.

As their child's first teacher, a parent is a teaching partner in the classroom and we need to acknowledge the teaching they are already doing. When talking with parents, the intentional teacher needs to ask about the favorite things parents are doing with their children at home and ask them to identify what they think their child is learning. This can be done while informally talking to parents about what they did on the weekend. The teacher may need to offer the parents examples of the skills and concepts their children are learning when they cook together or set the table, sort socks, or similar chores.

In addition to acknowledging the important ways parents are already supporting their child's learning, the intentional teacher can supply the following:

■ Take-home bags with books and activity ideas or books on tape. Use a small clear backpack or bag with handles. Include a book that relates to the theme or concepts being taught along with a tape of you reading the book.

■ Writer's suitcase — a small plastic case with a handle can house supplies such as pens, pencils, stencils, alphabet and number stamps, stamp pads, and paper.

■ Recipes for play dough or a favorite snack contained in a pocket folder or plastic holder accessible for parents to take as they leave.

■ Lending library of parent resource books located on a book shelf in the communication area that can be checked out.

A more formal two-way communication technique can be implemented by offering family conferencing opportunities at least twice a year. These conferences allow for trust to be built, increases mutual knowledge and respect, and allows sharing about the program, the child, and community resources. Ultimately, it will help foster good home-school connections. After you have described the child's strengths, interests, or abilities during the conference, you can suggest activities parents can do at home to extend the learning that is going on in the classroom. Supplying a handout of ideas that are specifically geared to their child is most beneficial. Informing them of the resources in the Parent Lending Library is also an Option. Simple activities that use readily available household items are best. Even everyday tasks like doing laundry or setting the table offer learning opportunities such as sorting, counting, matching, and learning new vocabulary. Keep the child's developmental level in mind when guiding parents to activities in resource books or with activities that you provide. You don't want them to become frustrated if the activity does not work or is at the wrong level for their child.

Communicate frequently with parents to find out if they are enjoying the extended activities at home. Sending an e-mail is an option if you don't get a chance to see them on a daily basis. If parents are not doing these extended activities, you might want to modify activity ideas or offer alternative suggestions. And of course, the more information you provide parents about their child's program or specifically about their day, the more inclined they will be to try to extend the activities at home, especially if they know the child enjoys block play, for example, or listening to books on tape.

In order to provide the best program for children and families, teachers need to be intentional in their communication with parents. Just as we can help children to learn, we can help adults to learn more about their children and be more intentional in their interactions with them. Providing parents with information on child development, activities to extend learning at home, and specific information about their child's interests and abilities will give them the tools to be more intentional with their child. And providing a space where they can access this information themselves as needed empowers them in regard to their child's educational experience. The result will be a meaningful learning experience for all involved and a positive start for children and families.

References

Bennett, T. (2007). *Mapping family resources and support: Spotlight on young children and families.* Washington, DC: NAEYC.

Epstein, A. (2007). *The intentional teacher.* Washington, DC: NAEYC.

Keyser, J. (2006). *From parents to partners: Building a family-centered early childhood program.* St. Paul, MN: Redleaf Press.

Stephens, K. (2007). *The Complete Parenting Exchange Library,* "Practical Advice for Parents on the Joys & Challenges of Contemporary Families." Redmond, WA: Exchange Press. Article is no longer available online.

Jody Martin

Jody Martin has a B.A. in Psychology and a minor in Child Development and over 25 years of extensive and diverse experience in the early childhood field. She has been a preschool teacher, a center director, and a curriculum manager. Currently, she is the Vice President of Education and Training at the Home Office for Crème *de la* Crème Early Learning Centers of Excellence. She has also authored articles for several early childhood publications and is a reviewer for several curriculum publishers. She is a dynamic presenter and recognized leader in the field of early childhood education with a commitment to providing quality programs for children.

The Demanding, Questioning, Over-involved Parent

That Would be Me

by Gigi Schweikert

It's been almost ten years, and four children later, since I wrote my first article about child care from the parent's perspective. Before having my own children, I had many jobs in the early childhood field — toddler teacher, director, toilet plunger — and I willingly, often without solicitation, distributed expert advice to parents across the country offering tips about how to put their children to bed, the best way to potty train, and why worksheets are taboo. Currently, I'm on a quest to retrace my early childhood encounters, seeking out every parent I ever gave professional advice to in order to apologize.

Why? Hey, some of the advice was pretty good! But what I never delivered with the directions for tantrum-prone kids or the ideas for children who wouldn't stay in bed was empathy, reassurance, or understanding. I stood on my developmentally appropriate soapbox with an indignant attitude of childrearing superiority. I made parents feel like failures with my any-idiot-can-do-this expert attitude and made hard-working moms and dads who were trying to juggle kids and the bills feel guilty. It wasn't my intention. I just never understood the day-to-day realities of being a parent.

Everyday Parenting

Now in the throes of everyday parenting and moving at mommy hyper-speed, I'll confess that what I say to parents and what I do as a parent, can be two very different things. Here are a few examples:

Advice: Ignore fellow shoppers when your child is having a tantrum in a store.
Reality: I'll run my Visa® card to the credit limit plucking things off the shelves in an attempt to find something to soothe my savage toddler, anything to help him be quiet.

Advice: Please label all your child's belongings, including socks.
Reality: Ever try to label an infant's sock? It's not big enough to write her name on. I'm just not up to sewing labels in socks small enough to fit a baby doll.

Advice: Kiss your child "good-bye," reassure him that you will be back later, and leave quickly.
Reality: I'm either sneaking out or staying until he stops crying, which will probably be around lunchtime. Separation is hard for me, too.

Advice: Children learn through play.
Reality: I'm not sure I want to pay all that tuition for my kid to play all day. When are you going to teach him to read?

Advice: Childhood is a journey not a race.
Reality: We may not like it or agree with it, but

today's world is really competitive. I want my child to finish the journey first.

Advice: Children who wear pull-ups, instead of underwear, may not toilet train as quickly.
Reality: That might be true, but pull-ups are a lot less messy. For the commute home, I'd put pull-ups on the whole family if they made them big enough for everyone.

Advice: Try to have your child to school on time to avoid disrupting your child's schedule and the school's activities.
Reality: It is not my intention to run my panty hose, run out of gas, or run off the road because of the constant bickering in the backseat; and I am always running late.

Advice: Children must be fever free for 24 hours before returning to child care.
Reality: Is that with Tylenol® or without? I prefer with.

'Us' and 'Them'

Like many of us in the child care field, I'm an 'us,' an early childhood professional, and a 'them,' a parent. As a professional, I'm usually rational, consistent, and solution oriented. But when it comes to my own kids, I can become irrational and emotionally driven. The thought of a conference with my three-year-old's preschool teacher can make my palms sweat. I'm convinced that whatever my kid's teacher has to say about the quality of his finger-painting skills and social interactions on the playground will definitely determine the fate of his Ivy League education.

While my 'us' side, an educator, writes articles about parenting on topics like discipline, nutrition, and limiting television viewing, my 'them' side, the parent, puts my kids in front of the television and hurls Oreo® cookies their way if one of my children approaches the computer so I can get my "expert work about parenting" completed. It's much easier to write about parenting than to be a parent.

So in the purest sense, an 'us' and a 'them' mentality is logical. Both sides, educators and parents, want

what is best for children, each working from a different perspective, one more rational, "It's not unusual for toddlers to bite," one more emotional, "Look at the bite on my daughter's face." Who's right? To a certain extent, we both are.

Beyond a Partnership: An Alliance

What's best for the child? We all know the answer to that: a constant alliance between the parent and the early childhood professional. The 'us' and the 'them' working together, sharing information and making decisions to determine the individual care and education of each child. But we do that, right? We try, but our parent partnerships are often no more than opportunities for parents to raise money for the playground or organize teacher appreciation luncheons. Which are not bad things, but an alliance requires us to listen to the advice of parents, not just for parents to listen to our advice. Let's face it, most of us like well-behaved, quiet parents and their well-behaved, quiet kids.

How can we give parents an opportunity to influence our programs? Ask them. Call a few parents each week just to ask them how things are going. Keep a checklist and call every parent at least once during the year. Have a two-minute written survey in the lobby and have parents write something they liked recently and something they would like to change. Call a parent whose children have graduated from your program and give them the same two-minute survey, "What did you appreciate about the school?" "Where could we make improvements?"

Beyond Child Care: Parent Care

Taking care of young children seems like enough of a job, taking care of their parents sounds impossible and why should we? It's good customer service for one; but beyond that, caring for parents promotes better parenting. Why not soothe a frazzled parent with coffee 'to go' after drop-off or have a place in each room where parents can put down their things as they settle in their child? Offer workshops based on parent interests. Limit the paperwork that goes home. Plan a school party in which parents don't have to bring anything. Make parking convenient. Send cards to parents for their birthday, promotion, new home, or new kid. Have extra diapers, extra milk, and extra bread on hand, so parents can skip a trip to the store. For parents who pull an occasional late pick-up, go ahead and feed their child dinner. We don't want to see parents fail any more than we want their children to fail. Everyone can use a little help — especially busy parents.

Beyond Tolerance: Acceptance

It's hard to love every child and even more diffi-cult to love their parents. With the hurried lives of some parents, we often wonder, "Why did they have children anyway?" I knew a parent who took a sales job and hardly saw his children. The wife was like a single mother. The father was always working and spent little time with his children. It was easy for me to judge his parenting as uncaring. I found out later that that dad grew up very poor and was determined to give his children a college education. That dad was my dad and all three of us, his children, finished college.

How little we know about the lives of the parents who come through our doors. Good programs have learned to tolerate seemingly inappropriate parental ways, like parents who spend too many hours on the job. But can we learn to accept parents knowing that the majority of parents work very hard to make a better life for their children?

Beyond Diversity: Inclusion

Janet Gonzalez-Mena and others have taught us to appreciate and celebrate the diversity of others. There has been a lot of progress in early childhood pro-grams. Most schools have baby dolls of many colors in the housekeeping area, musical instruments from around the world, and pictures on the walls that de-pict the richness of our society. But do our programs really reflect the many cultures of children and their parents? To really embrace diversity, we have to live it. Most days the smell of chicken fingers fills the air in our centers. We need center menus that include Asian, Indian, and good ol' Southern food; walls that are decorated with the art and tapestries of our school families; and practices that validate cultural differences such as the right age for toilet training and how often infants are held. True diversity is the inclusion of the cultural practices of the parents who attend our programs.

If we really want to value parents, to form an alli-ance, we have to understand who they are. At times, there is nothing rational or predictable about being a parent and their wanting the best for their child. We don't always know, nor do we need to know, the circumstances and lives of each parent. Hey, we'd all love it if the parents never complained, paid their tuition on time, listened to our advice, and did every-thing we said, since we are, in fact, 'the experts.' But as inconvenient as it may be, we should expect good parents to be demanding, questioning, and involved. Why? It's good for their child.

Gigi Schweikert

Gigi Schweikert is the working mother of four children and author of 18 books on parenting and early childhood education, including the best-selling *Winning Ways series* with Redleaf Press. With 25 years' experience, Gigi's practical ideas and realis-tic perspective on child care will have you laughing and learning. Gigi's an international keynote speaker, recently in Malaysia and New Zealand, and she'd love to come to your program, no matter where you are. She's on the advisory board of KidReports and believes technology can keep us connected.

Parent Meetings

Creative Ways to Make Them Meaningful

by Karen Stephens

Do you frequently complain about holding parent meetings because "hardly anyone shows up"? Does staff huddle up grousing that the parents who 'really needed the information' didn't even attend? Have you felt a little resentful about having to bribe parents into attending meetings by offering food and free child care?

If so, you're not alone. Many of us early childhood professionals get discouraged when parents don't seem as enthused about family enrichment opportunities as we think they should be. But if you are consistently seeing your parent relations cup as half empty, rather than half full, you and your staff need a bit of an attitude adjustment.

What kind of adjustment? First, re-define your criteria for a successful parent meeting. It's always easy to be disheartened by numbers, especially in the U.S. where we often judge success by size — big showy numbers denote achievement whether we're discussing our family incomes or our sports team's performance.

In our work, if we focus ONLY on numbers — namely how many parents attend any one meeting, we set ourselves up for disappointment. We also jump to some false assumptions.

For instance, if attendance numbers don't meet our expectations, we consider no show parents as less committed to or interested in childrearing. Assumptions like that undermine family-staff relations and most often are just not true.

Families are incredibly busy. Parents' full-time employment outside the home robs families of treasured time together. If we offer only night-time parent meetings, sometimes parents don't attend, not because they don't care, but because they care MORE about the time they actually have with their child. Can we fault them for that?

Overall, I consider a program a success if 10-25% of parents attend any one meeting. I also consider it a success if a variety of parents attend different meetings; rather than JUST having the same core group of parents attend. Variety means we are offering topics or events that appeal to diverse interests, rather than just a core group who think like us.

Encourage program staff NOT to take it personally when parents choose not to attend all your parent meetings. Like most of us, parents do what they can do — and they do what their conscience can live with.

MUCH more important than counting numbers is focusing on the quality of impact a meeting makes on parents' attitudes and behavior. With your staff, discuss what constitutes making a difference in parent's lives. Why are you offering parent meetings?

Discuss the fundamental goals for reaching out to parents. Is it important to us that parents establish friendships with each other and not just us?

If you focus on making a qualitative affect on even ONE parent, you'll be more encouraged. After all, don't we believe that impacting even one child's life can do a lot to create a better world? It makes sense also to believe that helping even one parent feel more competent, confident, or supported is a worthy success in our profession.

With that said, the remainder of this article will share a bevy of ways to make parent meetings successful — in a meaningful way.

Setting the Stage for Success

First things first. Below are some guidelines to keep in mind as you plan parent meetings.

Survey parents on what THEY want to learn about or discuss regarding childrearing or family life. Don't assume you know what parents want to know, or even need to know. Asking parents is respectful, and it helps you plan events that are responsive to their immediate needs.

Include parents in planning meetings. Strive for diversity and inclusion. Resist including only those parents who already seem to think like you do. Be sensitive to family culture when planning experiences.

Find motivating ways to get parents through the door. The best way is good word of mouth. The more fun, engaging, and meaningful meetings are, the more attendance will build. However, there are also other ways to motivate parents' attendance — some are inexpensive — other's not. Many programs offer door prizes or give parents a paperback children's book to take home. Offering free child care during a meeting is a great way to remove an obstacle to attendance. Rhonda Swanson, director of Northern State University Children's Center goes a step farther. She holds a raffle for a free day of child care. You might also consider bringing in a local celebrity occasionally, for instance a local newspaper feature writer or radio talk show host, who covers family issues.

Set the physical stage for success; creature comforts count. Plan for camaraderie and casual networking. And yes, offer food — even just snacks — to nourish the body as well as the mind. They sustain energy and are a cultural way of building a sense of community. (One year our kick-off parent meeting featured a pie buffet for a pie-tasting party. It was a fun icebreaker!)

Provide comfortable adult seating. Arrange seating for lots of face-to-face interaction among parents. Home-like, rather than office-like lighting and room temperature are helpful. Candles add warmth and ambiance, as can simple wind chimes or background music. Fresh flowers or a bubbling tabletop fountain contribute beauty and harmony. Such small things are easy to overlook, but they really do show parents respect and demonstrate that you value your time together.

Whatever you do, move away from classroom settings. For parents cooped up inside all day, a meeting room with windows reduces stress. If you don't have a parent lounge with comfortable couches and loveseats, consider reserving meeting space at a local coffee shop.

Occasionally vary the meeting day. While it's easier to remember a set monthly meeting date, it's harder for everyone to HAVE that particular day available. Occassionaly vary days to expand parent options for participation.

Vary the meeting times. Most programs plan meetings immediately after closing time so families don't have to go home and come back. That also requires serving a supper during a meeting for parents and the children in child care. But sometimes, offer lunch-time meetings for those families who really don't want to give up evening family time together. A breakfast meeting at a local café is another option.

Put technology to work. Think about a meeting of the minds rather than just physical face-to-face meetings. For some parents, discussing a topic with staff and fellow classroom parents online via a chat room is a preferred meeting method. At the very least, it can allow follow-up discussion to a parent meeting. Also offer a parent lending library with video- and audiotapes. You can then hold parent discussions on a particular tape several parents checked out, or ask a parent to write a newsletter review of a tape they viewed.

Intentionally include fathers as well as mothers. A great start is to ask some fathers to help plan or even facilitate a meeting.

Allow enough TIME for parents to process dialogue and information. Pace meetings for plenty of reflection, hands on activity, and discussion. I'm convinced that guiding and supporting parents through self-reflection and a parenting decision-making process is far more important than inundating them with facts and pressuring them to competently perform specific parenting skills.

Plan for ADULT learning styles. Find ways for parents to present and apply their unique expertise/ insights/experience. Vary activities to include all learning styles for adults. Think hands-on and speak to all the multiple intelligences. Lecture less; coach, facilitate, ask reflective questions MORE. Encourage PEER learning and support rather than dependence on an expert presenter or staff person. Generate alternatives rather than dictate advice or quick fixes.

Infuse training with unexpected creativity, uniqueness, and fun. Employ a variety of methods of presentation or discussion. Use jokes, cartoons, props, guest speakers, dramatic play, peer discussion.

Provide short and jargon-free take-home materials and handouts. These help parents to refer back to information, and they help them share ideas with those who co-parent with them, whether it be spouse, partner, or grandparent.

Meaningful and Creatively Engaging Parent Meetings

From bubbles to pebbles to children's books and poems, I use lots of different tools to encourage groups to open up and discuss issues. The props are often purchased at the local party store or handmade. I choose props based on how they might engage thought, symbolize a specific concept, engage hands-on involvement, and/or spark fun and relaxing conversations.

Other people hold different types of meetings to entice parents. Some sponsor formal parenting classes, such as STEP (Systematic Training for Effective Parenting). Others are less formal. For instance, Candice York, director of the University of Northern Iowa Child Development Center, reports hosting art fairs, game nights, and 'silly suppers' where kids and parents make suppers out of what are typically considered breakfast foods. In our program we hosted a "Trading Places Night" where everyone came to play typical classroom activities, but the children were the 'teachers' and the parents were the 'children.' It really helped parents respect children's learning and gave them a child's eye view of developmental skills encouraged through play.

Obviously, there are as many ways of offering parent meetings as there are directors. Below are some specific ideas I've found successful with parent groups. I hope they inspire you to find your own creative ways of reaching out to and working with parents.

■ **What's parenting like for you?** Ask parents to pair up in twos. Provide a hand-held toy microphone. Ask parents to take turns interviewing each other about the rewards — and yes, challenges — of parenting. Inevitably, parents will get to know each other better. Most importantly, they'll learn they are not alone in a lot of their parenting experiences.

Variation: Pretend you're filming a segment of a morning talk show. Ask parents to volunteer to be on an interview panel for a specific topic. For instance, how about a panel of parents talking about strategies for getting kids to bed on time — or for toilet training.

■ **Wish upon a star.** Give each parent a shiny cardboard star and a marker or pen. On one side of the star, ask them to write down (or draw a picture of) their hopes for their child. On the other side, ask them to write down or draw their dreams for their family. After writing/drawing is finished, ask parents to share their hopes and dreams with each other. Discuss specific ways for achieving our hopes for our children and dreams for our family. At meeting's end, encourage parents to take their star home to share with their children. And they might want to hang the star in a window or post on the refrigerator as a reminder of their heart's desire.

Variation: Pass out magic wands to parents. Ask each to share what they'd wish for in terms of parenting. More patience? More time?

■ **Ever felt like a broken record?** Before parents arrive, have one of those old-fashioned vinyl records placed at each seat. (You know, the ones stored in your basement collecting dust.) Then discuss. For instance, has anyone felt like a broken record with the kids? In what ways? Why do they think kids need repetition or reminding?

Variation: Play a song that could be used to foster discussion. For instance, as parents come in, play the song "Can't Buy Me Love" by the Beatles, or "Imagine" by John Lennon. What can those songs imply for parenting? Can parents think of other song titles that could serve as a theme song for parenting?

■ **A wonder from childhood.** Ask parents to bring one special item that will reveal something special about their childhood. Suggestions might be a favorite book, toy, or nature item. Ask volunteers to share their item with the group. What made it special? What meaning does it hold? What items do they believe are special or full of meaning in their child's life and why? How can we help children find things to love and cherish in life?

Variation: Ask parents to bring in a favored photo from their childhood. Discuss what made the experience in the photo memorable enough to treasure. What childhood experiences do they hope their child will treasure?

■ **Bubbles for reducing stress.** Give each parent a miniature bottle of bubble solution and wand. (Often sold as wedding reception table favors at party stores.) Ask each parent to silently think of a parenting concern or minor worry from the day. Then blow bubbles together, imagining the bubbles carrying their worries away. Ask BRAVE participants to share their imaginings. As people share, how many are similar? Encourage parents to suggest productive ways for coping with the particular concerns expressed.

Variation: Balloon pop. Have parents share a worry, write it on a slip of paper and then put it into a balloon. Everyone can blow up their balloon and then pop their worries away. (While inflating the balloons, encourage deep, relaxing breathing — not hyperventilation.)

Variation: Bubble wrap hop. Give everyone a sheet of bubble wrap packing and a permanent marker. Each person writes a frustration on their bubble wrap and then jumps on the wrap to stomp the worry away.

■ **Connecting with childhood.** Give participants a set of questions related to childhood to reflect upon and answer. Ask them to share their responses with each other. How will their responses affect how they will parent? How will they influence what experiences they offer their own children? Sample questions:

• During childhood, where was your favorite place to be?

• Describe play activities and settings that fully engaged you, the ones you could do for long periods with no sense of time passing. What was it about them that maintained your full, extended attention?

- What places or spaces or persons relaxed you most in childhood? What and/or who calmed you most easily?

- What scared you most as a child?

- What experiences do you believe every childhood should include?

■ **Myth of the perfect parent.** For each attendee provide a party paper plate and a marker. For mothers, provide a Barbie® paper plate; for dads, a Superman® paper plate. Talk about what each person considered to be the perfect parent BEFORE they actually became a parent. Compare that image to the reality of day-in and day-out parenting. Is the standard of perfection realistic for a parent? Are priorities needed? What is most important to be good at as a parent? After discussion, ask parents to list on their paper plate those things they'd like to give up in their pursuit of perfection. For instance, perfectly made beds or a huge income? At meeting's end, everyone tears up their paper plates and throws the pieces into the air. Do shoulders feel lightened? How can parents be more gentle in judging themselves in the future?

■ **Tuning into children's needs.** Provide a variety of chimes in the meeting room — whether tabletop or hanging. As parents enter, encourage them to test out and play with the chimes. Begin a discussion on children's need for responsive parenting. The chimes can symbolize the need to tune into children's developmental stages as well as unique temperament, abilities, and interests. If you can afford it, send each family home with a chime for their home.

■ **A voice like no one else's.** Pam Tuszynski of First Presbyterian Church Preschool in Hollywood, California, asks parents in her program to dictate children's books to record for their children's use in the classroom. What a soothing thing to do for children! Making those recordings together would be a great parent event. Ask parents to bring one

of their child's favorite books to the meeting. After parents share the books with each other, provide a recorder so they can spread out in the room for a group recording session. Especially close groups of parents might team up to read different characters in each other's book choices.

So there you have it, a bevy of ideas to bring your program's families together for engaging reflection and discussion. I hope these ideas inspire your own creative juices as you reach out to the parents and children in your circle of care. Enjoy the connections and more importantly, savor the relationships that spring from them.

References

Stephens, K. (May 2005). "Meaningful Family Engagement: Just Imagine the Possibilities." *Exchange, 163*, 18-23.

Neugebauer, R. (2004). "The Many Forms of Parent Involvement." *Exchange, 160*, 68-69.

Stephens, K. (May/June 2001). "Ice Breaker Activities Guaranteed to Warm Up Groups." *Exchange, 139*, 7-10.

Karen Stephens

Karen Stephens, M.S. in education specializing in early childhood, began her career as a teacher in a preschool classroom in 1975. From 1980 to May 2013 she served as campus child care director and taught child development and early childhood program administration courses for the Illinois State University's Department of Family and Consumer Sciences. Today she writes from her home and enjoys occasional travel to deliver staff development training and conference presentations.

Mrs. Godzilla Takes on the Child Development Experts

by Janet Gonzalez-Mena

Parent education is of concern to most of us in early childhood education right now. Yet when we get on our high horse and decide to save the world through educating parents, we often lose our perspective — at least I do. So in order to help me keep my perspective, and perhaps help you do so too, I decided to take off my professional hat, put on my parent hat, and write my confession.

My confession goes like this: As a parent I'm a bit like Godzilla (a name I got from a child who couldn't remember Mrs. Gonzalez). I'm powerful and basically good, but blundering. I don't leave as much destruction in my wake as my namesake, but I leave my share. I leave a lot less if I'm not confronted with heavy artillery.

In the end, though, things are righted, the destruction cleared away, and everything comes out on a happy note. I haven't ruined my kids or anything, but you might think I was going to if you watched me in action sometimes.

Don't get me wrong — it's not that I don't have skills. I can be analytical, organized, thoughtful, sensitive, responsive, stimulating, and I can manage children's behavior with the best of them. But my skills as a parent are different from my skills as a professional. I am different with my own children than I am with

other people's children. When I'm parenting, I'm not in my professional role.

The concept of two roles became clear to me the first time I was in a teacher role in my son's preschool class. I was being wonderfully cool and professional in a conflict situation — a contrast to the high emotion I probably would have felt at home with my own kids having this same conflict. My three-year-old son tugged at my arm when the dust had cleared, asking, "Mommy, why were you talking so funny to those kids?" My professional voice and words had sounded funny to my child who was used to me as Mommy. No one else regarded my handling of the situation as peculiar. In fact, I remember afterward being praised by my head teacher.

The strange thing is that I like myself as Godzilla as much as I like myself as a professional, an expert. I defend my rights to parent in my natural, amateur fashion. I don't want to be an expert parent. And in my role as expert, I don't want to give the parents the message that they should be experts — or that they should learn the right way or the good way to do something.

I want to support them in the good things they are doing and help them look at the areas that they are dissatisfied with for the purpose of coming to their own decisions about what changes to make or how.

I don't think about this subject much until I run into conflicts — like a while back. A friend, who is an early childhood professional (some of my best friends are professionals), went on a ski trip with my family. We sat in the back seat with my four-year-old son, Timmy. The talk went something like this. Timmy would interrupt the adult conversation periodically. "Look — snow!" I would glance out and respond without a lot of thought and something like, "Yeah, we're getting higher . . . " and then my friend, knowing that my response probably didn't make much sense to him, would respond with an explanation of altitude and how that affected the snow level, modeling what I knew were better ways of responding to a four year old.

Very soon I got irritated. I know how to talk at a child's level, expand language, increase concepts, and even reflect feelings, interpret hidden messages. I wasn't doing any of those things right then. I was talking adult talk with my friend. I didn't need to be reminded that there are better ways to respond to children. Furthermore, my friend wasn't helping me as a parent — she was making me mad. (See, I told you I am Godzilla.) I wouldn't have minded if she hadn't seemed to be correcting me. I would have loved it if she and Timmy had been carrying on the conversation and I had been free to become part of the adult conversation going on in the front seat. But that wasn't the case.

Here's another example of professional approach versus parenting approach. At a recent staff meeting in the children's center at the college where I teach, we were talking about yelling at children. Well, of course, I don't condone yelling as an acceptable approach in programs. But when yelling at home was criticized, I had to disagree. Some of the healthiest families I know yell at each other. (And I confess that I've done my share of yelling at my kids at home.) I suspect it's more cultural than anything else — maybe also an individual means of expression. I've seen a lot of polite and quiet families who have smoldering undercurrents that never get dealt with and lots

of noisy, argumentative families who deal actively with their conflicts. In my role as expert, I would never tell a parent not to yell at his or her child. As a teacher trainer, however, I would and do teach other ways of communicating.

Don't get me wrong. I'm not opposed to parent education. I think parents need all the attention they can get. Parenting is a hard job and there is a lot to learn. But the learning comes about as parents feel respected, as well as supported, while they gain the skills that suit them — not particularly the same set of skills needed to work with other people's children in a program setting. They gain most from professionals who build their confidence, boost their self-esteem, and alleviate their guilt.

So as you go out on your crusade to improve parenting skills (which some of us do willingly and others of us are mandated to do by our funding sources), remember that the parent role and teaching role are distinctly different. There's no such thing as an expert parent (except for a few of those who have studied it, but haven't tried it).

We don't want parents to be professionals. We want them to be natural, spontaneous, effective human beings who respond to their children from their individual and cultural inclinations. We want them to be themselves, even if those selves are more like Godzilla than Superman.

Janet Gonzalez-Mena

Janet Gonzalez-Mena was a student of Lilian Katz, Magda Gerber, and Anna Tardos. Today she does consulting and training in infant-toddler care, parenting, and diversity work.

Sharing Developmental Concerns with Parents

by Craig Gibson and Robert Naseef

From day one, you suspected that something was different with Jake. One of 20 students in your class, Jake, age 4, was the only child who was showing signs of atypical development. When given opportunities for social play, not only were Jake's play skills not functional or purposeful in nature, but he showed little interest in engaging other children in any kind of social interaction. When he did show interest, he just watched, perhaps not knowing how to join in, and then drifted off by himself. Often, Jake could be observed isolating himself in the corner of the classroom, spinning the wheels of a car for long periods of time or lining up blocks in rows on the floor or towers. Communicatively, Jake's expressive language skills were limited, even though he had a big vocabulary. This left him unable to put words together to effectively express his wants and needs to adults and peers. Jake's limited skills in this area often triggered tantrum behaviors, as he was unable to communicate thirst, hunger, discomfort, or pain. Based on conversations you have had with Jake's parents in the past, they believe he may be a little late to develop, though their concerns do not go beyond that. And so you are conflicted. Do you express your concerns to Jake's parents, or simply keep them to yourself? As a dedicated and caring early childhood professional, you are keenly aware that this news can be absolutely devastating to a parent, sometimes regardless of how you approach the topic. Reluctance to be the bearer of bad news is just human, and anxiety about broaching the subject is natural.

When you have concerns about a child's development, there are effective ways to approach this subject with parents that are non-threatening and non-invasive. Keep in mind that early childhood professionals are not diagnosticians. However, we have a responsibility to effectively express our concerns to parents, and guide them in the right direction, should they choose to seek outside help for their child. Listed are strategies you can use from the moment you detect developmental concerns to the time you sit down with a parent to express those concerns.

1 — Collecting Data

First and foremost, it is important to informally assess the child through observation and data collection. Make note of the atypical behaviors that you observe throughout the child's day. Consider a broad range of strategies to assess and record your observations. A description of this informal assessment process should be shared with all parents when they enroll in your program. Parents should know that developmental monitoring and periodic updates in parent-teacher meetings are an integral part of the educational services that are being provided. You'll want to share through what methods, at what times, and by whom children are assessed, how findings are documented and shared with parents, and what would indicate the need for a formal assessment and how that would be handled. Documentation is important when assessing children of all abilities, but especially for those for whom you have developmental concerns. Be sure to include the child's strengths, as well as any deficits, observed. Keep in mind that you may need to get written parental consent prior to conducting a formal assessment on their child. In other words, you need to know the difference between formal and informal developmental assessments:

- **Informal assessment:** Writing down anecdotal notes about a child's behaviors throughout his day.

- **Formal assessment:** Assessing a child's development in one or more areas of domain using a specific assessment tool.

2 — Discussing Findings as a Teaching Team

Concerns with a child's development should be brought to the attention of the director as soon as possible, in most instances even before an informal assessment is conducted. Your program may have established protocol for how this is done; and your director has the responsibility for making sure policies are followed as well, ensuring that you are supported in your teaching role. The establishment of a child study team allows staff to share emerging concerns about individual children on a regular basis. Continually sharing concerns among staff members may generate discussion on possible intervention strategies that could be implemented in a given area

of concern. You'll want to keep the privacy rights of families in mind here. You should, therefore, refrain from discussing your concerns about a child with anyone who does not work with the child directly.

3 — Calling a Meeting with Parents

Once you have collected data and discussed your concerns with your program director (and other members of your teaching team), you will want to arrange a meeting with the child's parents. Face-to-face is the best way to request a meeting with a parent. If this is not possible, you can communicate with the parent via telephone. Try to avoid e-mail or other forms of written communication, as these messages are often misunderstood. When requesting a meeting with parents, state that you would like to discuss their child's progress and development. This is not the time to express specific concerns; this will happen during the meeting itself.

4 — Holding the Meeting

Meeting participants. When meeting with a parent to discuss developmental concerns, it is essential to include your immediate supervisor. She serves as a witness; this can eliminate any confusion about what occurred. The director also can act as a facilitator at the meeting, assisting you and the parents in communicating with one another. Parents and teachers both have important information about an individual child and her development to be shared in this meeting.

Meeting etiquette. Parents should be greeted warmly upon arrival at the meeting. The meeting is an opportunity for teachers and parents to connect as a team in caring for the child and all efforts should be made to make this happen. Gestures like making eye contact, offering a handshake, or giving a warm smile can help put parents at ease. The specific gesture is not as important as the intention of establishing rapport and helping to make parents feel comfortable in the environment. You want to appreciate who your families are and where they come from. Be sensitive to the fact that gestures are culturally based and what may be comforting to one parent may be interpreted differently by another.

Body language is also important. Do what you can to communicate your partnership with parents by avoiding seating arrangements that place you at one end of a table and the parents at another. Sit beside the parent and let this communicate that the parent is an integral part of the team in addressing the needs of her child. Invite parents' comments and questions from the outset. It may turn out that parents share your concerns. Acknowledge and reassure parents that behavior and skills can differ from one setting to another and that this is valuable information. Invite parents to share their child's achievements with you, the progress they have seen their child make, and the positive traits and qualities their children have.

Sharing concerns. Conversations with parents always should be presented as a two-way sharing of information, rather than as a process of your trying to convince them of something. Begin the discussion by talking about a child's progress: What she *can* do. Invite parents' active participation in the conversation by sharing what they have observed. Ask them what their short-term goals are for their child.

When it comes time to share the specific concerns you have about their child's development, remember that you are simply sharing your observations, you are not drawing conclusions as to *why*, your hypothesis about what could be happening, or a diagnosis of any kind. It is important to remember that families and educators both can help make sense of and address the behavior or skill deficits that are of concern, and that the ultimate decision to pursue additional support/evaluation rests solely with the parents. When sharing your concerns with parents, it is a good idea to show them photographs, video clips, completed checklists, anecdotal data, and/or other specific examples that best illustrate the concerns you have. This allows everyone to understand more precisely what is being described and encourages parents to share similar (and different) examples, as

well as to offer their own insights into what is being shared.

Suggesting next steps. Once you have discussed your concerns with parents, you will want to suggest possible avenues the parent could take in getting help for their child. Start by telling the parent about early intervention, which, according to the law that created it, is: "a statewide, comprehensive, coordinated, multidisciplinary, interagency system that provides early intervention services for infants and toddlers with disabilities and their families." The goal of early intervention is just that — to intervene early, in one or more areas of developmental concern (www.first-signs.org). Let parents know that early intervention is voluntary and it is entirely their choice to pursue these services.

If they choose to explore this option and give their consent, a team of early intervention specialists would evaluate their child in all developmental domains (e.g. cognition, communication, social/emotional, physical, and adaptive behavior). Upon completion of their evaluation, the team presents their findings to the family and offers their conclusion about whether the child is demonstrating any delays. If delays are detected, the team (e.g. parents, early intervention specialists, classroom teacher, program administrator) come together to discuss and agree on goals and services for the child.

Parents play an important role in this process as they are the experts on their own child. Their input is critical to the process. Parents should understand that the purpose of early intervention is not to diagnose children, but to provide them with supplemental services within the context of their early childhood program (e.g. services are often rendered in inclusive settings). If the parents would like to seek a formal diagnosis for their child, they would need to schedule an appointment with their developmental pediatrician, or other specialist such as an audiologist.

In Conclusion

As you can see, whether your concern for a child is based on a suspicion of autism or something else, the process for sharing these concerns with families is the same. Any anxiety you have about doing this is normal and natural. Parenting is a passionate relationship. No parent wants something to be wrong with their child. On the other hand, people will be grateful that you truly care and want to help them find the help their child needs. Most parents will be receptive to what you have to tell them, once it is clear that you have the best interests of their child at heart. Sometimes parents are not receptive to what you share with them because they are not ready to hear it and to consider the implications for their child and their family.

It is a privilege to be invited into families' lives in the way that we are. We must always respect the distinct roles each of us has in the partnership and to be supportive of each other when the conversation is a potentially difficult one like this.

Craig Gibson

Craig Gibson is a certified teacher in the state of Pennsylvania who has worked in a variety of academic settings, primarily with the special needs population. In addition to working in both public and private schools in Maryland, New Jersey, and Virginia, he worked as an early intervention teacher in Philadelphia, Pennsylvania, and is presently employed as the lead evaluator for a non-profit agency in southeastern Pennsylvania. In addition, Craig advocates for parents of special needs children, and enjoys giving talks to parents and professionals who have children or students with developmental delays. Craig holds bachelor's and master's degrees in Elementary Education and Special Education, respectively. He has published numerous journal articles and is a regular contributor to *Exchange*. Craig is the Editor-In-Charge of AutismSpot.com, and SensorySpot.com.

Robert Naseef

Robert Naseef is a psychologist and father of an adult son with autism. His new book, *Autism in the Family: Caring and Coping Together* (2013) includes advance praise from Temple Grandin: "Fathers often have difficulty expressing their feelings, and this book should be required reading for all fathers who have a child with a disability." *Special Children, Challenged Parents: The Struggles and Rewards of Parenting a Child with a Disability* (1996) has received international recognition. He has lectured internationally and appeared on radio and television. He is the co-editor of *Voices from the Spectrum: Parents, Grandparents, Siblings, People with Autism, and Professionals Share Their Wisdom* (2006). *Living Along the Autism Spectrum* (2009) is a DVD that features him, along with Stephen Shore and Dan Gottlieb. In 2008, he was honored by Variety, the Children's Charity for his outstanding contributions to the autism community. Visit him on the web at www.alternativechoices.com and listen to his insights about fathers who are raising children with autism at www.youtube.com/watch?v=1r3W-RScxR4.

Parental Anger

Causes, Triggers, and Strategies to Help

by Roberta J. Wilburn

The role of an early childhood educator is a complex one. We must wear many hats if we are going to be effective in working with the children entrusted in our care. Although the children are our primary focus, it is important for early childhood educators to understand the significant role that we play in the lives of the parents and other family members associated with our children. We take ownership for 'our children,' as we affectionately like to call the children enrolled in our classes; however, too often we dissociate ourselves from the most important people in their lives, their parents. When we embrace the concept of educating the whole child, we must also embrace the concept that in order for us to effectively work with the child, we must also be able to effectively work with their parents.

As teachers we are often the first ones to notice problems in parent-child relationships; therefore, it is important that we realize the critical role we can play in assisting families in resolving issues and getting the help that they need. However, sometimes instead of being a positive support for the families of our children, we choose to pass judgement, assign blame, and do little except complain to others about how we can't understand why Mrs. Smith treats Johnny so badly. Let's examine some alternatives to helping children and families who may be having problems.

According to Ron Huxley (2002), anger is one of the most commonly reported problems in families today. In a study of 285 'normal' parents, two-thirds indicated feeling anger to the point of shouting or screaming at their child an average of five times per week (McKay et al., 1996). Anger is an emotion that we all experience from time to time and it is normal for parents to get angry at their children. The problem arises when a parent becomes so overwhelmed with anger that they respond in abusive, unproductive, and destructive ways. The question is what can teachers do to identify parents who may be having problems expressing their anger in appropriate ways and what strategies can be used to help both the parent and the child?

Causes of Parental Anger

Parental anger can be caused by many different things. Usually the parent is already stressed and emotionally vulnerable when a particular incident takes place that acts as a trigger and causes the anger reaction to be released. Rarely is there just one thing that causes an anger episode, but rather a series of events that push the parent to her limits. Then something takes place, which tips the scales and makes the parents' anger go over the edge. Any one situation may not be problematic; however, when several factors come into play, it makes the parent emotionally vulnerable for explosive anger reactions. When a parent's personal resources are exhausted, they are more likely to become angry. Anger is usually a signal that something in the life of the person needs to be changed. Some of the common causes of parental anger include:

Groups of Parents At-risk for Excessive Parental Anger

Certain parent groups are at a greater risk for experiencing problems with anger management than others due to stressful life circumstances. Stress is a major contributing factor that cause frequent and problematic parental anger reactions. Some of the groups that are most vulnerable are:

Parents of children with disabilities — The birth of a disabled child can be a very traumatic experience for parents. These parents go through the grieving stage described by Kubler-Ross and anger is the third stage in this process. Kroth (1985) states that since taking out their anger on a disabled child is not socially acceptable, very often these parents take their anger out on each other, and others around them, including the child's teacher. Caring for a child with a disability can be extremely demanding, particularly if there is a lot of medical involvement. This can produce a significant amount of emotional and financial stress on the family. This stress can cause tempers to be short, which can lead to frequent and intense anger reactions in parents. If parents are trying to discipline their child during an anger episode, the intended discipline can escalate to abuse. The statistics concerning child abuse and children with disabilities are staggering. Turnbull and Turnbull (1997) reported the following:

■ Children with disabilities experience abuse at a rate 1.7 times higher than did children without disabilities.

■ Children who have disabilities experience emotional maltreatment at a rate 2.8 times more often than did children without disabilities.

■ The incidence of physical abuse among abused children with disabilities was 9 per 1,000, or 2.1 times the rate for abused children without disabilities.

■ Among abused children with disabilities, the incidence of sexual abuse was 3.5 per 1,000, or 1.8 times the rate for sexually abused children who did not have disabilities.

■ Among abused children with disabilities, the incidence of physical neglect was 12 per 1,000 or, or 1.6 times the rate for abused children without disabilities.

Parents going through divorce — Divorce is another stress-producing situation, which can predispose parents to excessive anger reactions. Situations where one parent is strongly against the divorce can create intense feelings of anger and rage in the parent who feels they have been wronged. This anger can be targeted at the other spouse, the child, the teacher, or anyone else who the parent may feel is taking sides against them. Dr. Rhoades (2002) states that in a divorce, typically both sides regress into angry and vindictive behavior. Parental Alienation Syndrome (PAS) sometimes occurs as a result of a parental anger and is used to get revenge against the other parent. A person with PAS will try to alienate the child from the custodial parent by falsely alleging child abuse. Approximately 50% of child abuse allegations in divorce proceedings are falsely raised.

Teen parents — Teen parents are also at-risk for having problems with anger management problems because many teens have unrealistic expectations about what it is like to have a baby. Teens believe that a baby is going to be like a doll that can give them unconditional love. When the reality of having a baby hits them and they find out that babies are messy, they cry a lot, and demand a lot of attention, which takes them away from enjoying many of the activities of their peers, they become angry. Anger may also surface when the teen has difficulty consoling their child or when their child is not able to do the things they expect them to (i.e., toilet training — they don't like changing diapers so the teen parent may try to toilet train their child at an inappropriate age before they are developmentally ready. When the child wets himself, the teen parent may become angry and use excessive punishment to try to get the child to comply with their expectations).

Parents who were abused as children, have experienced domestic violence, or other traumatic experiences — Child abuse has a cycle effect. The majority of the children who were abused end up abusing their own children when they grow up and become parents, particularly if they never got any help to resolve issues related to the abuse. "Those parents who hope to be different from their own parents may find that they are prone to the same problems" (Galinsky, 1987). Some of these parents find that their anger toward their child can be as strong as their intense love for the child. Since children learn how to deal with their emotions by the behavior modeled for them (even if they were not abused themselves, but were raised in a home where domestic violence was a way of life), it will become apparent in their pattern of interacting with others. Also, parents who may be victims of domestic violence or victims of other traumatic events may take out their anger and sense of powerlessness by exerting their aggression and rage on others who are smaller, weaker, or more vulnerable than they are.

According to Parkinson (1993), anger is a very common and natural reaction to trauma and loss. This anger can be directed at anyone including themselves. The extension of the parent anger is the need to blame someone for what has happened to them.

Parental Stress That Can Trigger Anger Reactions

Research has found that there are two elements that always precede an anger episode: stress and trigger thoughts (McKay et al., 1996). Common things in the life of a parent which may bring about stress include the following:

■ The long and demanding responsibility of parenting can be very stressful.

■ Young children require that parents spend a lot of time and energy cleaning up, picking up, and supervising.

■ It can be difficult for a parent to find a moment where they can have peace and quiet to engage in such things as reading, talking on the phone, meditating, or even going to the bathroom in peace.

■ Young children are egocentric. Most of the time they aren't aware that you are tired, you had a bad day at work, and you need a few minutes to yourself. They want you to be interested in what's going on in their life at that moment and if you don't respond, they may become increasingly demanding or whiny depending on the age of the child.

■ As young children strive for autonomy and independence, they tend to test limits and question their parents' judgment and authority. This not only brings about a source of stress, it also can cause conflict and power struggles between parent and child, depending on how the situation is handled.

■ Young children need a lot of attention and are constantly seeking approval from their parents. This tremendous need for attention can cause them to use a variety of attention-getting strategies; some are appropriate and some that aren't appropriate. Both can be equally stressful on a tired and overtaxed parent.

■ Young children require constant supervision to protect them from immediate and potential dangers. This need for constant vigilance on the part of the parent can be very taxing, particularly when the parent has a very active and/or high energy child.

Anger reactions or episodes occur because a parent may already be stressed, frustrated, tired, or overwhelmed by life's circumstances and their child does something, which becomes "the straw that breaks the camel's back," and it triggers parental anger. Child behaviors which often trigger parental anger reactions are as follows:

■ Child's behavior defies or tests the parents' authority and makes the parent feel as though he is losing control.

■ Problem behaviors that were considered minor, begin to escalate.

■ Child's behaviors remind the parent of their own shortcomings and inadequacies which may trigger negative memories.

■ Child becomes excessively demanding, noisy, or messy.

Certain behaviors can trigger anger reactions in parents, but many times what actually triggers the anger reaction is not the behavior itself but what the parent thinks the behavior means. These thoughts are called trigger thoughts or selftalk. Trigger thoughts transform unbearable levels of stress into anger (McKay et al., 1996). Trigger thoughts and self-talk fuels the fire of anger and prolongs the anger long after the incident is over (Weisinger, 1985). Let's look at the following scenario:

Several things caused Mrs. Jackson's anger episode. The first problem that contributed to the anger episode was that Mrs. Jackson was already stressed out due to the break-up of her marriage and concern about whether she would financially be able to support her family. Mrs. Jackson was already in an emotionally vulnerable state. Tameka's behavior (yelling and not letting her leave) was the primary trigger that set the anger episode in motion. The secondary trigger that caused the anger episode to escalate to the point where it was out of control, was Mrs. Jackson's thoughts (Tameka is deliberately doing this to me to embarrass me and to get her way). These thoughts added fuel to the fire and caused Mrs. Jackson to respond with excessive anger. If Mrs. Jackson had realized that Tameka's behavior was a result of her fear of abandonment and rejection resulting from her parents' separation, she probably would have responded differently to her child. The anger episode may never have occurred or may not have reached the level that it did.

In a study of parental anger conducted by McKay et al. (1996), 20 child behaviors were identified that

Mrs. Jackson never used to have any problems dropping off four-year-old Tameka at school until recently. Now, every day going to school is a major battle. At night Tameka tells her mom about all of the fun things they did at the center during the day. She even tells her mom about the things she is looking forward to doing the next day, but when they arrive at the center door, things change. Today was the worst. When Mrs. Jackson and Tameka got to school, Tameka started crying and grabbed her mom's arm and started screaming, "Mommy don't leave me, don't leave me." Mrs. Jackson tried to free herself from Tameka but she just got louder and louder. Then Mrs. Jackson finally got loose and she grabbed Tameka's shoulders and started shaking her while screaming, "Why are you doing this to me?" This continued until the teacher came over and intervened.

Mrs. Jackson confided to the teacher that she doesn't understand why Tameka is doing this to her. She said Tameka is just being manipulative and deliberately trying to embarrass her in order to get her way. The reality of the situation was that Mrs. Jackson and her husband had recently separated, and Tameka hasn't seen her dad in three weeks. The Jacksons did not tell Tameka why Mr. Jackson wasn't going to be living with them any more because they felt she was too young to understand. Tameka loves school but is afraid that if her mother leaves her, she won't come back, just like her dad. The last time Tameka saw him was when she left for school one day. When she came home he wasn't there as ususal, and she hasn't seen him since that time.

frequently evoked high levels of anger in parents. They found that what makes these situations more upsetting to parents were their own trigger thoughts. These thoughts made the situation seem worse than it was because trigger thoughts are usually based on faulty assumptions, which are magnified or blown out of proportion and result in the parent viewing the child and his behavior in a negative way. Look at the following example of how trigger thoughts can cloud a parent's perception of a situation:

Behavior: Child interrupts parent while she is talking with another adult.

How parental trigger thoughts cause the parent to view the situation:

Assumed intent: You are doing this on purpose to annoy me.

Magnification: This behavior is intolerable.

Labeling: You're a disrespectful brat.

Real cause of the behavior: Child needs more attention from his parent but because of his age, has a difficult time delaying gratification and knowing how to get it in appropriate ways.

How the parent's anger reaction makes the problem worse: The parent repeatedly scolds the child for interrupting. This actually reinforces the child's behavior. Even though the interactions between the parent and child are negative, the child is getting attention. For many children, negative attention is better than no attention at all. When the parent interrupts the child talking, she is modeling the same behavior she finds intolerable. Both of these parental actions are likely to cause the problem behavior to continue and possibly increase. Every time the behavior continues, the parental trigger thoughts are reinforced and increases the likelihood that the next parental response to the child's interruptions will be an anger episode of greater intensity.

The level of parental anger can be significantly reduced if teachers can help parents to replace their trigger thoughts with a greater understanding of her child's temperament, age-appropriate behaviors, need for belonging and significance, and the role of reinforcement. Since trigger thoughts are a major contributor to the occurrence, level, and intensity of anger episodes, if we can help parents change their thinking patterns we may be able to reduce the number and frequency of anger-triggered interactions between parents and children, as well as enhance their relationship. Teachers can help parents change their thinking patterns by helping them understand why their child behaves the way he does and to develop more realistic expectations for his behavior.

How to Tell if a Parent Has an Anger Problem

Since all parents experience and display anger at some point during parenthood, how can teachers tell if a parent's anger is out of control and should be considered a problem? Dr. Hendrie Weisinger (1985) has identified five indicators, which can help you determine if a parent has an anger management problem. These indicators have to do with the intensity, frequency, and impact on interactions with others. If you have a parent who you believe is having difficulty with anger, you can use the five indicators below to assess whether you should try to assist the parent with getting help in dealing with their anger:

- Anger episodes occur frequently.

- The anger reactions are often intense or at high levels.

- Parental anger lasts for a long period of time after the initial incident took place.

- The anger reaction leads to verbal or physical aggression.

- Parental anger negatively impacts the child, the parent-child relationship, relationships with teachers and other parents, or cause disruption of classroom activities.

The frequency and intensity of the anger episode is very significant. Intense anger leads to verbal and physical abuse of others. Research has found that the frequency and intensity of parental anger is strongly related to the use of physical punishment. When the parent tries to use physical punishment during an intense anger episode, it is highly probable that what started out as punishment will result in abuse. McKay et al., (1996) found that anger-driven corporal punishment is a risk factor in abuse. Child abuse is the leading cause of death in children of the United States. Approximately 12 children a day suffer brain damage from abuse. A 1994 Gallup Poll found that 1 in 20 parents discipline their children to a point where they commit physical abuse.

Recognizing Warning Signs

In order to help parents who have problems with anger management, it is helpful if you learn to recognize warning signs parents may exhibit prior to their anger getting out of control. When a person becomes increasingly agitated, it affects his behavior. An observant teacher should be able to notice several changes in a parent's behavior, which may signal that their temper is rising. Some of the warning signs you can watch for are:

Tips for Teachers

- Teachers need to be careful not to interact with parents in such a way as to cause parental anger to escalate (i.e., don't argue with the parent, don't raise your voice, and don't blame the parent).

- Don't become defensive.

- Don't belittle or minimize the problem.

- Look for early warning signs and provide support for parent before things get totally out of control.

- Remind parents that it is normal for parents to get angry with their children from time to time, but it is important to control the anger and not let the anger control them.

- Do not talk down to the parent or try to patronize them.

- Don't promise parents things you can't produce just to keep them quiet.

- As the parent speaks more loudly, you speak more quietly.

- Actively listen to what the parent has to say.

- Do not discuss the parent's problems with other parents. Remember personal information shared in confidence should be kept confidential unless it is a matter of child abuse. In such cases the information should be shared with the center director and reported to the appropriate authorities.

- Develop a list of parent resources (i.e., local parent support groups, anger management classes, magazines and articles with parenting tips).

- If the above strategies are not working and the problem persists, refer the parent for professional help.

■ Volume of the parent's voice increases. As a person becomes increasingly angry, the volume of their voice also increases.

■ The conversation shifts from pleasant to abrasive or comes across as a verbal assault.

■ If you look at the parent's hands, his fists may be clenched.

■ If the parent gets upset over something that would normally not be a problem.

■ Look at the parent's facial expression for signs of agitation such as tight jaws, frowns, scowls, flushed.

■ Listen to the parent's tone of voice and what she is saying (i.e., ranting and raving, cursing, blaming, insulting).

Impact of Parental Anger on the Child

Parental anger can have a significant impact on the development of young children because it is through the interactions with parents and other significant adults in the lives of children that they shape their view of themselves, others, and the world around them. Children learn how to deal with their feelings and emotion by observing how their parents respond. If a parent is having difficulty dealing with his anger, then it will be difficult for the child to learn appropriate ways of managing her own anger.

Prolonged exposure to parental anger can also have long-term effects on the child, which he may carry into adulthood. Adolescents and adult children of parents who had anger problems often experience problems with delinquency, depression, alienation, limited career and economic achievement, and problems with interpersonal relationships. These children also find that when they become parents, they also have problems in expressing anger in appropriate ways (Colglazier, 2002).

Strategies to Help Parents Deal With Their Anger

As teachers we can provide help and support for parents who may be experiencing difficulty with anger management. Some strategies that you might find useful in working with parents with anger problems are listed below. Encourage parents to do the following:

■ Change their thinking patterns

■ Identify their trigger thoughts and avoid negative self-talk

■ Take personal responsibility for their anger (you can not control what another person does, but you can control how you respond)

■ Find safe and healthy ways to vent their anger

■ Increase their social support network

■ Take a mental and physical time-out away from the situation that caused them to get angry

■ Avoid drinking or using drugs when they become angry

■ Do something physically constructive when they become angry, such as walking, jogging, or cleaning.

■ Take time to reassess the situation that made them angry before they respond

■ Self-monitor their anger episodes (i.e., how many times a day/week do you get angry?)

■ Tune-in to their bodies; when they notice body changes which indicate they are becoming agitated (i.e. spasms, knots in stomach, headaches, increasing voice volume), they need to take steps to calm down

■ Be aware of high-risk situations that trigger anger reactions

■ Clearly convey their expectations to their child and be consistent in seeing that the child adheres

References and Resources

Colglazier, T., "Understanding Your Anger Management." www.childhoodresources.com/article1019.html Article is no longer available online.

Galinksky, E. (1987). *The six stages of parenthood.* Reading, MA: Addison-Wesley Publishing, Company.

Huxley, R. "Anger Tools for Families." www.angermanagementgroups.com/anger-tools-for-families

Huxley, R. "Top Ten (Non-Abusive) Parenting Tools." www.parentingtoolbox.com/tentools.html Article is no longer available online.

Kroth, R. (1985). *Communicating with parents of exceptional children.* Denver, CO: Love Publishing Company.

McKay, M., Fanning, P., Paleg, K., & Landis, D. (1996). *When anger hurts your kids: A parent's guide.* Oakland, CA: New Harbinger Publications.

Parkinson, F. (1993). *Post-trauma stress.* Tucson, AR: Fisher Books.

Rhoades, G. "Questions and Answers about Anger." www.anger-management.net/about.html Article is no longer available online.

Turnbull, A., & Turnbull, H. (1997). *Families, professionals, and exceptionality.* Upper Saddle River, NJ: Merrill.

Roberta J. Wilburn

Dr. Wilburn is currently Associate Dean of Graduate Studies in Education & Diversity Initiatives at Whitworth University, and has over 30 years of experience in higher education in the subjects of Teacher Training, Counseling, Cultural Awareness, International Studies, Early Intervention, Early Childhood Education, and Family Support Programs. She holds an Ed.D in Early Childhood/Special Education from George Washington University and her Th.D in Christian Counseling from Jacksonville Theological Seminary. Dr. Wilburn has served as Chair of the Division of Education at Lemoyne-Owen College, as well as a professor of special education at the University of Memphis, Howard University, and Delaware State College. Most recently, Dr. Wilburn was awarded the NAACP Service Award by the Spokane Chapter in 2013. "My vision is for equal access to high-quality education for all students in Washington regardless of their race, ethnicity, socioeconomic status, gender, or cultural group," said Dr. Wilburn. "The learning opportunities in our state should be as diverse as the students we serve; with programs that are intentionally designed utilizing innovative, differentiated, instructional strategies based on sound pedagogical principles."

the Art of
LEADERSHIP

ENGAGING FAMILIES
IN EARLY CHILDHOOD ORGANIZATIONS

3

CHAPTER 3

Working with
All Types of Families

Working with Non-traditional Families

by Lisa Eisenbud

Single parents, stepparents, grandparents as parents, foster parents, same-sex parents, racially-mixed children and families, families formed through adoption. . . . What does the increase in numbers and varieties of non-traditional families mean to you as a child care center director? It challenges you to learn about these families, and how your child care can be a positive force in their children's lives.

Parents in non-traditional families, like all parents, want their children to be happy and healthy and to grow up to be the best people they can be. They want the same high-quality care as other parents, but have an added concern about an environment where their families will be respected and their children taught the value of diversity.

The Parents

The tools to help you meet your goal of doing what's best for non-traditional families start with good communication skills. However, with non-traditional parents this can be a bigger challenge requiring more finesse than usual. You are in the position of needing personal family information before you have the time to really build up a relationship with the parents. Many of these non-traditional parents, particularly those who are a different ethnicity than their children, may continually be asked prying, insensitive, insulting questions from nosy acquaintances and even strangers regarding their families. Therefore, they may be guarded about answering questions about their children and sharing personal information. Likewise, parents may be reluctant to be forthcoming for fear they will be judged, or that their children will be treated differently by staff. In addition, family stories may be painful, as with grandparents raising their grandchildren or families involved in bitter divorces. A director needs to make the parents/guardians feel comfortable enough to discuss their family situations.

Let prospective parents know, from the very start, that you are not just accepting of diversity, but that you are a center that embraces and celebrates all families. Do this not just by talking about your philosophy, but by how that philosophy translates into the classroom and educates the children about different families; the activities you do, the books on the shelves, taking advantage of everyday situations

Note: The word parent in this article refers to any adult who plays a primary parenting role.

to talk about all differences, teacher trainings on diversity. . . . Most importantly you want to communicate that children will be in an environment that lets them know, in many different ways, that their families are valued.

Reassuring parents that you are a center that understands the importance of supporting all families can go a long way in helping them feel comfortable sharing information. Phrases such as: "We strive to be inclusive and teach children that there are different types of people and families"; "We have a variety of different families at our center and we think it is important to get to know them"; "Learning about our families helps us get to know the children and how we can best support and help them develop as people"; "We are very proud of our commitment to teaching children about diversity and acceptance of all differences." Explaining why it is in the child's best interest for the adults around him to be aware of his family situation can help convince a parent to share important information. As director, you have the chance to put parents at ease and give them the message that you are their ally — that you care about their children.

Confidentiality and professionalism are also important messages to convey to nontraditional parents. Assure families that their family information will only be shared as a means to enable staff to meet their child's needs in learning the lessons of family diversity. Let them know that any information parents feel the director or certain staff should know, but want kept private, will be.

Nevertheless, even your best efforts may not always be successful in opening up a parent. In such a case you and your staff will just have to do the best you can in supporting and caring about the child and family. Over time, as you build a rapport, the reluctant parent may become more comfortable sharing information. By continuing to be supportive and letting parents know you are there for them, you leave the door open.

The Children

In some cases, children in non-traditional families have been through traumas that will affect their transition into your child care, as well as their behavior. In others, the non-traditional family make-up will not have any overwhelming affect. Even within the same family types there are differences. For example, single-parent families can be formed due to death, incarceration, abandonment, single parent by choice, or a guardianship situation. Children of divorce or those being raised by their grandparents have obviously had some sort of trauma in their lives. However, the situation of a child being raised by grandparents whose parents died when he was a baby is very different from a child who was taken away from a drug-addicted mother at age three. Likewise, a child born into a two lesbian-parent family has very different life experiences than one whose mother and father divorced and then one of them realizes he or she is gay.

Keep in mind, even children who go through the same situations may react differently. Do not fall into the trap of stereotyping and generalizing about children from non-traditional families. It is a misconception to automatically assume there is a problem, or when there is one, to blame it on the non-traditional family make-up. As with all children, any problems require assessment of every possible contributing factor.

In many instances your child care program may be the children's first experience with the world outside their loved ones. Your reactions to their families will affect their identity and self-esteem. Along with lessons in cultural, racial, religious, and physical differences, you can help children as they come to realize that families can be different. Every child benefits from learning that there are all different types of families and what matters is that they are loved and cared for.

A major goal of early childhood education is to teach young children that we all have differences as well as similarities. The challenge is to teach that differences should not be seen as negative, or something to be ashamed of, but something to be proud of and celebrate. Learning that families can look different, but also have much in common, can help teach the important lesson of acceptance.

Your Staff

It is your staff who will be most impacted by these children from non-traditional families. They will be the ones asked the difficult questions: "Why is Alfred's skin brown and his mommy's is white?"; "Where is Amy's mommy and daddy, why does she live with her grandparents/foster mom?" What will your staff say to this scene: Two girls are playing dress up and pretending to get married. A boy comes over and says, "Two girls can't get married, you have to marry a boy." One girl, whose lesbian mothers taught her that there are all kinds of marriages, replies, "Yes, two girls can get married; my moms are girls and they are married."

Teachers have the power to open children's minds and hearts to accepting differences, to help them feel good about their families and themselves. "There are all different kinds of families; in some families everyone has the same skin color, in other families they have different skin colors. What's important is that everyone in a family loves one another." "Amy's mommy and daddy could not take care of her, so she is very lucky to have her grandparents/foster mom who loves her very much and takes such good care of her." "People believe different things about marriage so there are different kinds of marriages."

It all starts with attitudes and values about non-traditional families. You and your staff need to talk about and examine your own feelings about these families. Can a teacher who believes homosexuality is wrong be welcoming and embracing to a family with lesbian or gay parents? Will a teacher's quality of work be affected if she thinks divorce or choosing single parenthood is wrong? Teachers need to educate themselves about the different types of families to find the many similarities between them, as well as the issues and concerns that may be unique to a particular family in their class.

Do your teachers feel comfortable asking parents questions and speaking with them about their families? How do they feel when talking with the children about different families? Perhaps you need to do some training to help those who are less comfortable or less experienced. Showing teachers that the same kinds of language and teaching they use to teach children about other differences can be used for family diversity. The goal in answering the questions, "Why doesn't Sam celebrate Christmas?" and "Why does Sam have two dads?" are the same: respect for and acceptance of differences.

Having staff meetings with family issues on the agenda gives you a chance to share information in a professional manner and not on-the-fly where confidentiality can be breached and information missed. It is a good idea to have a plan for sharing information with all staff including afternoon shift teachers and substitutes. Think about who needs to know if there are custody and pick-up issues? Who needs to know if a child is from a non-traditional family?

Adding families to your agenda on a regular basis is a good way to ensure information does not fall through the cracks, everyone is updated on what they need to know, and teachers have a forum to discuss any family related issues or concerns.

The lessons learned in your program become instrumental building blocks in the foundation upon which children's self-esteem, identity, and trust in people are built. Children are impacted, either negatively or positively, by teachers' attitudes towards their families. What teachers say, how they say it, and whether the lesson of family diversity is woven into the everyday world, or merely reserved for Family Week sends a message.

One of our jobs as early childhood professionals is to help children make sense of the world and their place in it. Children look to the adults around them for approval and acceptance. Having teachers who not only think they are great, but that their families are great, too, can go a long way toward a strong foundation of self-esteem that will serve your children well for the rest of their lives.

Some suggested questions to help you get at the information you need are:

All Non-traditional Families:

■ Tell me about your family?

■ What is your child taught at home (about her race, about having gay dads . . .)?

■ What has your child been told (about parent in jail, about drug-addicted parent . . .)?

■ What can staff do to support what is being taught at home?

■ How long has your child been in the present situation (how old was your child when adopted)?

■ Are there any custody or pick-up issues we need to be aware of?

■ What other adults play a parenting/important role in the child's life?

■ What are the parents' concerns?

Single Parent:

■ Is there a mother/father in the child's life? In what way?

Step/Blended:

■ What does your child call his stepparent? Stepgrandparents?

■ Are there stepsiblings?

Gay/Lesbian:

■ What does your child call each parent?

■ Are both parents legally the parents? (Programs need to know this for medical emergency.)

■ Is there a father/mother in your child's life? In what way?

Grandparents/Other Relatives/Foster Parent:

■ Where do you stand legally? (Programs need to know this for medical emergency.)

■ What does your child call grandparents/relative/ foster parent?

■ Is there any contact with biological parents? What kind?

■ If applicable, any known affects from drug abuse/ neglect?

Suggestions for Embracing All Families and Teaching the Value of Family Diversity:

■ Treat grandparents/guardians/lesbian and gay non-biological parents as parents

■ Pictures and posters on the walls depicting all types of families

■ Teach tolerance sticker displayed

■ Forms that say parent/guardian not mother/father

■ Family of origin and sexual orientation included in your nondiscrimination statement

■ Learn what children call family members and use that language

■ Books depicting family diversity, diversity in general, friendship, feelings, self-esteem

■ Get rid of out-of-date books and wicked stepmothers

■ Use natural classroom situations to talk about different families and all differences

■ Integrate various families into your language and every day play (two moms, two dads, adoption, stepdad...)

■ Teach children about feelings, empathy, and accepting differences

- Bulletin board ideas: Our Families, Who Cooks Dinner At My House, What I Like To Do With My Family

- Make "All About Me", "All About My Family" books

- "How are we different, how are we the same" game: Teacher names two or three children and they think of things that are different and the same about them.

- Have variety of play people for your doll house to represent a variety of families

- Be sensitive during holidays, ask parents what would be appropriate

- Encourage parents to visit, read, do an activity, come on field trip

- Find out what you can do to help their child

- Emphasize to the children that family is the people who love and take care of them.

The lessons of diversity should be ongoing strands woven throughout your curriculum that constantly evolve and grow. Seek out resources for more and different ideas and ways to incorporate them.

Bibliography

Children's Books:

Gordon, S. (2000). *All families are different.* New York: Prometheus Books.

Kroll, V. (1994). *Beginnings: How families come to be.* Morton Grove, IL: Concept Books.

Pellegrini, N. (1991). *Families are different.* New York: Holiday House.

Skutch, R. (1998). *Who's in a family?* Berkeley, CA: Tricycle Press.

Simon, N. (1987). *All kinds of families.* Chicago: Albert Whitman & Co.

Simon, N. (1993). *Why am I different?* Chicago: Albert Whitman & Co.

Books for Adults:

Crumbley, J. (1997). *Relatives raising children: An overview of kinship care.* Child Welfare League of America.

De Toledo, S., & Elder Brown, D. (1995). *Grandparents as parents: A survival guide for raising a second family.* New York: Guilford Press.

Doucette-Dodman, D., & Lacure, J. (1997). *Raising our children's children.* Minneapolis, MN: Fairview Press.

Drucker, J. (1998). *Families of value: Gay and lesbian parents & their children speak out.* New York: Insight Books.

Funderburg, L. (1994). *Black, white, other: Biracial Americans talk about race and identity.* New York: W. Morrow and Co.

Kaeser, G., & Gillespie, P. (1997). *Of many colors: Portraits of multiracial families.* Amherst: University of Massachusetts Press.

Register, C. (1990). *"Are those kids yours?": American families with children adopted from other countries.* New York: Free Press.

Schooler, J. E., & Keefer, B. E. (2000). *Telling the truth to your adopted or foster child: Making sense of the past.* New York: Bergin & Garvey.

Watkins, M. (1995). *Talking with young children about adoption.* New Haven: Yale University Press.

Wright, M. A. (1998). *I'm chocolate, you're vanilla: Raising healthy black and biracial children in a race-conscious world.* San Francisco: Jossey-Bass.

Lisa Eisenbud

Lisa Eisenbud, MS, has been a toddler teacher, a center director, a family resource and referral counselor, and is presently an early childhood consultant in the Boston area. She facilitates workshops for child care professionals as well as parents on a variety of topics. "Working With Non-Traditional Families" is one of her specialties. Lisa is also the program coordinator for Parenting Resource Associates, overseeing 100 workshops a year.

Supporting Multicultural, Multilingual Families

by Julie Garrett

Karen D. Love is a very special site located in the Linda Vista area of San Diego, California. We are a Head Start program funded for 162 children; we provide services from 6:00 am until midnight. The Love Center covers a large block on the corner of Drescher and extends to Tait Street. Our environment provides a warm, welcoming space for a diversity of parents and families who enter our classrooms as it encourages personnel growth. The environment represents the joy and passion of the 100 languages of all the children, parents, and teachers.

I transferred to Karen D. Love almost three years ago. When I first arrived at the center, I was unaware of the large size of the site and staff I was going to be responsible for. As I toured the grounds, in my heart I wanted everything to change quickly, especially the classrooms and the outdoor area. It took time for me to admit to myself that this was going to be a long process, and that what I needed the most was patience and the true faith that it would be different by the time the children and families arrived in September. I began to dream of how I always felt as a teacher, that if I ever supervised a center I wanted it to be the greatest of the greatest. I wanted the children, families, and staff to enjoy the environment where they were to spend their time.

I began to get to know my staff, shared some of my ideas, and asked them for their input and support.

My supervisor and I had already worked on environments at another Head Start center where I taught for four years; we both knew we wanted to explore our ideas beyond what we had done before. We started cleaning, scrubbing, and selecting equipment and materials to make all classrooms inviting for our children and families.

The first class we set up was for the full-day and the evening programs. When the children walked into the new room they were so excited! They thought a fairy had come overnight and changed the classroom, and they actually wanted to stay in that room. This was a pleasant surprise to us because that room was originally called the 'nightmare room.' The beauty of the new environment created a space for the children to value and enabled them to communicate with each other. It has had a great impact on how both the children and the parents experience the program.

The parents are now very involved in their child's education. Parents are bringing their younger children to the program; children who have gone on to kindergarten and first grade frequently visit us. They love to come back and see the teachers and let them know how they are doing. The teachers are awesome! Our staff is a great team and I respect the passion of each teacher.

As I visit the village daily, I can see specific ideas teachers are using as well as their exploration and deep passions for the children and classrooms. They have created an environment that is interactive and creative; an environment that encourages and provokes wonder, socialization, and a place to heal. The teachers are respected and feel free to express their creativity. It is wonderful to have such great people who care and enjoy their environment. We grow together and focus on the message we want to give to people when they walk into the center.

Environment Supported by Families, Community, and Partnerships

At the Love Center, diversity is a key element we consider when organizing and planning the use of different materials. We plan an aesthetic environment reflecting the community culture, language, and ethnicity of the children and families. Appreciation and respect is shown to each child by listening and responding to their family culture and lifestyle, which is integrated in a natural way.

Parents feel welcome in the physical environment and are involved in a variety of ways. By recognizing that their child's independence is linked to their trust, development, and confidence in themselves and others, parents are able to support our teachers daily regarding the child's strengths, interest, and learning styles. This gives parents and teachers a chance to develop strategies together. Our parents and staff work together supporting and respecting the home language, cultures, and family composition of each child in a way that supports their health and well-being. The classroom provides books and materials that reflect families' home languages and cultures as well as the community.

Parents and teachers have captured the creative experience by using cardboard, picture frames, mirrors, shelves, cameras, and documentation boards displayed in the art gallery. As you enter the classrooms on Tait Street, your eyes are able to capture the image of the children. You see work done by the children on canvas, benches designed by the children, and painted rocks around the water fountain.

Our journey continues as we work with the community, building partnerships with University of San Diego students, La Jolla Country Day School graduating senior class, San Diego Church of Christ Global Outreach Program, and Job Corp students to improve the outdoor area of the Love Center. Adding grass to the majority of the sand areas, wood chips around the climbing structure, flowers along the sides of the building, and painting buildings have all improved the community environment, providing a more comfortable space to explore and create a sense of ownership. Parents and students are involved in special projects to make our center beautiful. They volunteer on the weekends and throughout the week continuing to paint, weed, and plant flowers.

Visual and Written Expressions of Art

The children go on field trips to explore the community, visiting a number of businesses located within walking distance of our center. The children have done special projects by documenting in family albums our trips to the flower shop, fire department, post office, bank, local grocery stores, and library.

Children continue to enhance their creative activities as lighting and a stage are added to their dramatic play area. Many of their conversations are captured through recordings that are transcribed and posted for parents and teachers to read, thereby extending dramatic play and literacy activities in the language of the children.

Miniature objects are used by children to increase their ability to identify rhyming sounds. The teachers and children have set up an extensive music area with musical instruments, both purchased, and class-made. Under the observation of their teachers and parents, the children are experimenting with various musical instruments and writing down their compositions in a music journal. Later, the children may perform their song for their classmates. They are developing an understanding that writing is a way of communicating for a variety of purposes.

As we continue our projects throughout the Love Center, the children, families, and community volunteers are clearing the grounds of weeds as they begin to plan and plant their annual garden. They are enhancing their scientific skills by using clipboards, art paper, and pens to collect and record gardening data. This year they expanded their gardening experiences with the addition of sunflowers, pansies, and daises, as well as carrots and string beans. The growing cycle is documented weekly in the children's journals, expanding their ability to observe, describe, and discuss the natural world, and leading to a greater visual and written expression of art.

The families through the center are focusing on a variety of ways to share their culture. Children were curious about what their parents' lives were like before television and computers. The children were surprised to learn that families spent time singing, playing games, and making quilts together. This led to many discussions about how their families spent their days and the necessity of making household items from used material. The children learned that families saved scraps from old clothing to create quilts and pillows, not only to keep them warm but also as an expression of art. These quilts were often handed down from generation to generation and sometimes told stories. This led to sewing bees, a group of parents and neighbors who came together and sewed a quilt based on their environment and life experiences. The children, parents, teachers, and University of San Diego students continued dialoguing with each other. The children created their own sewing bee community. They drew self-portraits on muslin material using fabric markers. The adults observed and documented the children's conversations with each other as they attached their squares to the quilt using a sewing machine donated by one of our grandparents in the classroom.

The children have gained the ability to use various art media and materials in a variety of ways for creative expression and representation. The drawings are more detailed than previous work. Parents and teachers have captured the creative experiences on film and designed documentation boards. The quilts and pillows are on display in the art gallery for viewing. Another surprise for the children was the fact that their teachers had never made a quilt before; they were co-learners with the children.

During a classroom evening parent meeting, the parents in Room 3 came up with a great idea of sharing different cultures by making documentation boards. By making these documentation boards they were able to share their languages, family portraits, food, clothing, and family history in a multicultural gathering. The gathering involved the children visiting the local supermarket and purchasing food to prepare in the classroom. The parents created a great bond with each other and the teacher during this special event.

The children are demonstrating an awareness and respect of the differences and similarities among each other and other people, which in turn is helping them understand cultures, language, and family structures that are different from their own. Our site represents a high-quality program model for visitors in the child development field from different schools and colleges throughout the county of San Diego. In September 2001, Karen D. Love became a demonstration site for Neighborhood House Association.

Julie Garrett

Julie Garrett has been in the field of Child Development for 16 years with the Neighborhood House Association (NHA) in San Diego, California. She began as a teacher in 1985 working at a variety of sites in the agency. In 1999, she assumed the position as a center director at Karen D. Love Head Start and has held the position for the past three years. Karen D. Love became a pilot program practicing the Reggio Emilia Approach in 1999. In addition, Julie's site has been a demonstration site since 2001. Her site is responsible for training teachers, associate teachers, family service assistants, custodians, and center directors.

Today's Families:

Who Are We and Why Does It Matter?

by Lisa King and Kirsten Haugen

Today's families are more diverse than ever, and early childhood programs may be the first place a child or family will share who they are with the wider world. This puts early educators in a unique position to engage our growing diversity in ways that positively impact young children's sense of self and sense of belonging. In this article, we aim to briefly describe the rapidly shifting and expanding diversity of modern families, and at the same time, look beyond labels to appreciate the often unexpected and unique strengths, challenges, experiences, and perspectives of individual children and families.

We share insights from conversations we've had with several families about their own experiences, every one rich with joys, frustrations, and more. Their stories and perspectives illustrate the complexity of today's families. They compel us to go beyond helping children 'fit in' to instead strive for ways to learn about, incorporate, and leverage what is unique about each child and family, and to create a trusting, welcoming, and accepting community for parents, children, and teachers that will continue to evolve with each new child and family we meet.

A Word on Language

Lisa writes:

On a typical day at our house, two of my boys, ages 9 and 10, argue over whether or not a 'contest' and 'competition' are the same. I suggest they consult that authoritative tome of our common understanding of the words we use: our big, old, red *American Heritage Dictionary* of the English Language from my college days. As usual, this only leads to more arguing over synonyms, antonyms, and the like. They carry their dispute and their skateboards outside, and I get back to work on this article. The abandoned dictionary beckons, and I flip to the following entry:

fam·i·ly — n., pl. — lies. Abbr. fam

1. The most instinctive, fundamental social or mating group in man and animal, especially the union of man and woman through marriage and their offspring; parents and their children.

2. One's spouse and children.

3. Persons related by blood or lineage.

4. Lineage; especially upper-class lineage.

5. All the members of a household; those who share one's domestic home.

Time for a new dictionary! A quick look at Yahoo.com delivers the following, coincidentally from the current *American Heritage Dictionary*:

fam·i·ly — noun: pl. fam·i·lies

1. A fundamental social group in society typically consisting of one or two parents and their children.

2. Two or more people who share goals and values, have long-term commitments to one another, and reside usually in the same dwelling place.

3. All the members of a household under one roof.

4. A group of persons sharing common ancestry.

What a relief to learn that over the last 30 years, the definition of family has broadened to recognize families like ours and ones we've introduced in this article. Recent research reveals that young children already have an even more sophisticated understanding of family (Cohen et al., 2007):

■ They recognize there are many different types of family structures.

■ They give family a social rather than a biological meaning.

■ They see family more in terms of significant relationships than close blood relatives.

Diversity is the New Norm

"In my family, what I want people to know about me is that I'm adopted. We were all adopted. The only one who wasn't adopted in my family is Daddy."
— Mason, middle schooler

"What is the gay lifestyle? It's about getting the laundry done and figuring out what's for dinner every day."
— Stephen and Rudy

"We've moved around a lot and seen more than just what's here. Laural and I are opposites, in a way. She was raised by a single mom. I have two stable, married parents. We're a large family . . . five kids. We've got the mixed-race thing, and I'm a veteran. We're just normal people. Everybody is unique." — Brian

"We are a bilingual, bicultural family. We've lived in the United States and México. Our children went to preschool in México. They've always spoken English,

but did not use it academically until we came here."
— Ellen

"I'm 73, and my husband is 71, and we've been parenting our grandchildren. My daughter is an addict. . . . After a long period of treatment and recovery, she's doing well, but her youngest remains with us and only spends weekends with her mom. We're fortunate to have our family close. We feel grateful to be able to help." — Sherry

"The rest of my family is in Kansas. And even in Kansas, the surprising thing about my family is not that we're lesbian, but that we're vegetarian!" — Leah

"I am from two families."
— Lauren, elementary student

"There are so many ways to describe our family. We never know what's going to be on the front burner."
— Lisa

Family diversity comes, not surprisingly, in all shapes and sizes, origins, colors, and combinations (see sidebar: Diversity Data). The children and families who share their stories with us are not unusual. Some may face some significant challenges, but all are basically getting by or doing well. Experiences have included divorce, single parenting, immigration, learning English, grandparents as caregivers, sandwich generations, special needs, adoption, fostering, step-family blends, military deployments, homelessness, disabilities, parents or offspring who are lesbian, gay, bisexual or transgendered (LGBT), religious minorities, and more.[1] Beyond that, these and all families are fluid — continuously touched and reshaped by illness, death, separation, divorce, the addition of family members, economics, and other caregiver-related changes. We can no longer think of each instance of diversity as an exception.

Acknowledging and accepting this growing diversity and fluidity of families can challenge our own experiences, and our beliefs or attitudes about what makes a family and even how to teach young children. Doing so requires us to stretch, sometimes in uncomfortable ways, to communicate more and take more risks. It also gives us the opportunity to create environments that are welcoming to all, where children and families are invited to help build community rather than being asked to 'fit in.'

What We Do Matters

"Before Ilsa started preschool, it was like living in a big cocoon. With preschool, it was like, this is the start of coming out of the cocoon." — Kirsten

Most children who come into our care already have a sense of belonging in their families. Our job as early educators is to help them carry this over into their social identities. The images, words, and representations of families in media, books, and even in our daily language have not changed as rapidly as reality. Trumbull and Pacheco (2005) report, "There are countless ways that children in 'traditional' nuclear families have their reality mirrored back to them. Kids in other kinds of structures often feel invisible or even ashamed."

Handed-down assumptions about children, families, and learning that pervade our culture and institutions require that we make a conscious effort to truly shift our views and actions to pay attention to the messages we send to children and families through our words, expectations, images, and learning materials. Hollins (1996) notes that with few exceptions, the culture of American schools represents a system of beliefs, values, and practices that reflect the implicit values of the dominant U.S. culture, which in turn influence how students interact with each other, how teachers and students interact, and how the rewards system is organized (Trumbull & Pacheco, 2005). This unconscious, dominant perspective is more visible and at times more daunting to families who do not fit the traditional mold.

Looking Beyond Labels

Understanding demographic shifts is a beginning, not an end, to understanding the diverse experiences of the children and families we work with.

"Some things about our family are visually obvious, such as both parents are women, we are older than most parents with kids our age, and our family is interracial. Other things are not as obvious: we are Jewish, vegetarian, and very committed to nonviolent conflict resolution." — Clare

"I'm Swedish. My husband is African American. My children are surprised when people think they are black. They see themselves as mixed, and both sides are important to them. We don't really understand what all the fuss is about." — Susanne

"In the military we used labels all the time. It was a way to dehumanize others. It made people less than what they were. We need to see beyond descriptors to understand people more three-dimensionally, to have successful relationships." — Brian

"The biggest thing I want people to understand is we are a committed two-parent family. Whoever sits at the dinner table every night doesn't have to have a specific sex. We may look different on the outside, but we want our children to be respected, cared for, and loved." — Kirsten

Unexpected Strengths and Challenges

Some differences have inherent challenges. It's simply hard to live in poverty, to face a health crisis, or to manage in a new culture or with a new language. But keep in mind, other differences present challenges that arise or are amplified by cultural norms or expectations. Furthermore, what challenges some families may be a non-issue or even a strength or source of pride for others. When families differ from the norm, they may be able to think more deeply or broadly about who they are. They may be more aware of or in tune with things going on behind the scenes. And through it all, their 'insides' are far more complex than their 'outsides.'

"I'm a single parent. My parents, who live separately, do much in providing overnight care and in getting my daughter to daycare in the morning when I have to be at work. We have support from friends in town, too. My daughter is well loved and cared for by many people." — Frannie

"Because of our own experience, we are more conscious of race and how it affects all people and what race means in different parts of our community." — Beth

"Because of the differences we have, we have more . . . openness? We are more respectful of others who have differences. Because there's a parent with a disability in our family, I think it makes us more comfortable with others who have disabilities." — Leah

"We are sensitive to how differences are portrayed in the media, and in society, because the messages that are sent are often about us. And they are often wrong!" — Lisa

"Our strength is that we have love, respect for each other, structure in our family, and strong moral values." — Leah

"It's a challenge getting used to people asking us questions and learning how to answer or deflect them. Maybe that's a strength, too, because we get opportunities to talk to people about family." — Beth

"I am a wiser and better parent now than I ever would have been in my 20s, or even 30s, so I do think there are advantages to being an older parent." — Frannie

What Families Want

"I would like educators to find out as much as possible about each and every child in their classroom, about their unique culture and family situation. I would like them to help foster an understanding and accepting environment where all kinds of families are discussed regularly in a very natural and open way, and they are celebrated. A place where the diversity of people and ideas are also discussed, valued, and incorporated into the school day." — Frannie

"Categorizing and labeling are natural. It's how we process the world around us, but I'd like educators to find out more — what's beyond the label. If we could say it out loud and talk openly about assumptions — get to know the people behind the labels. . . . I want people to become more self-aware of their own assumptions when seeing our family." — Clare

"I want educators to be more patient and more open-minded about other people's cultures and traditions. A teacher respected our religious event. That was important to me." — Amsatou

"Please respect my family by getting to know each of us." — Beth

Educators have many opportunities to regularly re-examine and revise ways to develop meaningful relationships. The way the intake process is organized, the language we use, and the way the classroom materials are chosen and presented matters. Celebrating a child's 'Adoption Day' or addressing letters to parents/guardians/caregivers, for example, recognizes and normalizes the diversity of today's families. The families we spoke with were touched by many things educators have done to recognize that there are differences, and that beyond being special, those differences are just normal. These actions help our children know that they continue to belong.

Making a Difference

"Our preschool is always respectful of differences. They bring multiple views into the classroom through books, materials, and music. They recognize what's important to the kids and are comfortable talking about everything." — Beth

"In preschool the teachers would make sure when talking about families that they had books, pictures on the wall, stories that were appropriate, and showed a wide variety of families. It was great how they would — what seemed like incidentally — mention families with differences. Not centering on it, but naturalizing differences." — Leah

Our preschool attempted to find a Cinderella story from every country of origin for each kid in the classroom." — Frannie

"My second grade teacher was nice and she was interested in my West African origins." — Fatou, middle school

"Finding the balance between marginalizing and addressing differences is not easy. We need special treat-

Reflecting on Families

That's a family: Watch the trailer for That's a Family, a documentary aimed at children in kindergarten to fifth grade. Use the teaching guide to consider the messages and opportunities it inspires: groundspark.org/our-films-and-campaigns/thatfamily

Family fluidity: Describe your own family today, five years ago, and five years from now. Families are fluid, not static. What events have changed the structure of your family, its needs, attitudes, or resilience?

Imagine a family: What image comes to mind when you hear the word family? Who is in it? What do they look like? Does your image shift if you add the word *adopted*? *Special needs*? *Multiracial*? *Immigrants*? *Divorced*? *Gay or lesbian*? *Homeless*?

Just Google it: Try searching the web for images of 'normal American family' or 'happy American family.' Then try adding different demographic descriptors into the search. How do the results change? Are the images positive? Accurate? Up to date?

Look at the families portrayed in advertisements: What family structures, belongings, and values do these images promote?

Up a (family) tree?: Does the family tree still work as a metaphor for the way families form? We've heard people talk of the family constellation, the modern family, the organic family, the nuclear family, and the family quilt. Can any single phrase encompass the wide variety of situations that real families are experiencing?

Mirrors and windows: Explore how another family is both similar (a mirror) and different (a window) to your own. (groundspark.org/our-films-and-campaigns/thatfamily/taf_discussart). Do we . . .

- use what we know to make activities feel special for all children?

- work with families to build trust?

- avoid making families feel vulnerable or inadequate?

- work as a team with parents to solve problems?

- try to find out what families think is important?

- communicate in a variety of ways with families every day?

Family friendly?

As a staff, use the questions suggested by Civian and Shannon (2004) to ask yourselves, Do we . . .

- use what we know to make activities feel special for all children?

- work with families to build trust?

- avoid making families feel vulnerable or inadequate?

- work as a team with parents to solve problems?

- try to find out what families think is important?

- communicate in a variety of ways with families every day?

Before beginning any classroom activity, review your materials with your current group of children in mind. How are the children included or excluded by the images, language, or process of the activities or materials?

ment. It's necessary for us for communication, which is a pretty basic need. In the day-to-day, we're just the same as anybody, but because of my partner's deafness, communication is much more important in our family than in others'. There are bigger consequences if something goes wrong. For example, the school can't just pick up the phone and call if they need Sharon. We need to plan ahead." — Leah

"Our recent homelessness was an unexpected challenge. We were living in a trailer in the back parking lot of the Friends Meeting House across from the school. The principal let us use a spare room in the building in the evenings for homework, and other things. We didn't have to ask. It was offered to us. That really helped." — Brian

"I said to the director, 'I know it's going to be really hard [to provide materials on time in Braille]. But do you want to know what's hard? Being a deaf-blind kindergartner is hard.' He got it, eventually. One thing I loved was when Lauren was invited to teach the kindergarten class about Braille. She was very happy to do it. They all wanted their names in Braille. It was her chance to be the expert and tell others something she's an expert about . . . ." — Sarah

Knowing that we can't predict what each family may want, need, or might offer, the way we respond to problems that arise communicates our beliefs. We are the messengers; we shape the evolving dominant culture. We are models of best responses.

"Roscoe wore his pink shirt and came home unhappy because some kids told him it was a girl color. After a quick email, the principal wore his pink shirt the next day!" — Lisa

"Instead of saying to a second-grader, 'We don't tolerate that kind of comment here,' they could use the comment as a discussion point." — Leah

In our experiences, some of the most positive things have happened when . . .

■ boundaries between home and school get blurred a bit: When the kindergarten teacher made a home visit before school started and plopped down on our less-than-sparkling floor to play Legos® or

when the third grade teacher wrote really, really thoughtful comments on a report card.

■ communication is open, personal and non-threatening. Teachers do not feel the need to be 'the expert.'

■ teachers and administrators offer flexibility within the expectations or requirements of both kids and families, including how families can contribute.

■ educators model some risk taking.

■ the child and family feel valued.

■ feedback is genuine and positive feedback is not false.

The common denominator is a willingness to get to know families as they are, rather than in comparison to a traditional norm, and an effort to build multiple open, genuine avenues of communication.

References and Resources

Addy, S., & Wight, V. (2012). *Basic facts about low-income children: Children under age six.* New York: National Center for Children in Poverty. Retrieved from nccp.org/publications/pub_1054.html

The Annie E. Casey Foundation (2012). *Kids count: Data book.* Baltimore, MD: The Annie E. Casey Foundation. Retrieved from www.aecf.org/work/kids-count/?rules=2

Bassuk, E., & Friedman, S., et al. (2005). *Facts on trauma and homeless children.* Los Angeles: National Child Traumatic Stress Network. Retrieved from nctsnet.org/nctsn_assets/pdfs/promising_practices/Facts_on_Trauma_and_Homeless_Children.pdf

Brau, M. (2010). *Americans with disabilities: 2010.* Washington, DC: U.S. Census Bureau. Retrieved from census.gov/prod/2012pubs/p70-131.pdf Article is no longer available online.

Chasnoff, D. (2005). *That's a family!* (Video). San Francisco: Groundspark. A documentary on family diversity, which includes extensive training materials, recommended for kindergarten through grade five. Available in English and Spanish from groundspark.org/our-films-and-campaigns/thatfamily

Child Trends. (2012). Children with special health care needs. Retrieved from www.childtrendsdatabank.org/?q=node/332 Article is no longer available online.

Diversity Data: A Snapshot

- "Family living arrangements and trajectories are increasingly varied and complex in the United States. Age of marriage is at an all-time high. Cohabitation, not marriage, is the typical first type of union in U.S. society. Divorce and remarriage remain common, and births to unmarried women have accelerated rapidly, from 5% in 1960 to about 40% today" (Olson, 2011).

- More than four out of ten adopted children (43%) lived with their birth families at some time prior to their adoption (Vandivere, Malm, & Radel, 2009). Adopted children are less likely than are children in the general population to live in households with incomes below the poverty threshold (12% vs. 18%), and more likely to be read or sung to by their parents (Vandivere, Malm, & Radel, 2009).

- As of 2010, nearly one in four children in the United States is the son or daughter of an immigrant. Seventy percent of these children are American citizens. These young Americans will make up at least 25% of our new workers, parents, and voters for the next two decades (New American Children). Also in 2010, 22% of children ages 5-17 spoke a language other than English at home, up from 18% in 2000. One in 20 children have difficulty speaking English (Wallman, 2012).

- As of 2010, approximately one in 12 children had a disability, half of those being severe disabilities. Most disabilities are cognitive in nature (Brau, 2010).

- About one in seven children in 2009-2010 had a special health care need, according to their parent's report (Child Trends, 2012).

- "In 2010, 22% of children ages 0-17 (16.4 million) lived in poverty. This is up from a low of 16% in 2000 and 2001." One in ten children lived in homes with incomes below half the poverty threshold (Wallman, 2012).

- Families now make up 40% of the U.S. homeless population. "The typical homeless family is headed by a single mother, usually in her late 20s. She has with her two or three young children, typically preschoolers" (Bassuk, Friedman et al., 2005).

Racial and ethnic diversity has grown in the United States . . .

- By 2023, less than half of all children are projected to be white, non-Hispanic. By 2050, 39% of U.S. children are projected to be Hispanic (up from 24% in 2011), and 38% are projected to be white, non-Hispanic (down from 53% in 2011 and 62% in 2000) (Wallman, 2012). Children who identify with two or more race groups are projected to make up 5% of all U.S. children by 2050 (up from 4% in 2011) (Wallman, 2012).

- One million gay and lesbian parents are raising two million kids in the U.S. (Family Equality Council, 2012). Same-sex couples with only adopted or only stepchildren have significantly higher incomes than both married and unmarried opposite-sex households. Four percent of all adopted children in the U.S. are being raised by gay or lesbian parents (Gates et al., 2007).

Civian, J., & Shannon, L. (2004). *What is family-friendly child care and why does it matter? What parents and providers say — and the implications for quality care.* A research study funded by the IBM Global Work/Life Fund and conducted by WFD Consulting. Retrieved from http://abcdependentcare.com/docs/Family-Friendly-Project-Final-Report.pdf

Cohen, S., et al. (2007). *Family diversity: A guide for teachers.* Nicosia, Cyprus: Second Transnational Exchange Programme. Retrieved from www.csca.org.cy/doc/Family%20Diversity%20Guide,%20English.pdf

Gates, G. J., Badgett, M. V. L., Macomber, J. E., & Chambers, K. (2007). *Adoption and foster care by gay and lesbian parents in the*

United States. Los Angeles: The Williams Institute, UCLA Law School.

Hollins, E. R. (1996). *Culture in school learning: Revealing the deep meaning*. Mahwah, NJ: Erlbaum.

Kreider, R., & Elliott, D. (2009). Poster Presentation: *The complex living arrangements of children and their unmarried parents*. Detroit, MI: Population Association of America. Retrieved from census.gov/hhes/socdemo/children/data/cps/complex/complex-abstract.pdf

Krivickas, K., & Lofquist, D. (2011). *Demographics of same-sex couple households with children*. Washington, DC: U.S. Census Bureau: Fertility & Family Statistics Branch, SEHSD Working Paper Number 2011-11.

Levine, M. (2008). *The price of privilege: How parental pressure and material advantage are creating a generation of disconnected and unhappy kids*. New York: Harper Perennial.

Majors, S. (2012). Op-Ed: *Take a 'look-back' at what LGBT families look like*. Family Equality Council. Retrieved from www.familyequality.org/equal_family_blog/2012/11/13/1481/op-ed_take_a_look-back_at_what_lgbt_families_look_like

Migration Policy Institute. (2012). *Migration information source*. Washington, DC: Migration Policy Institute. Retrieved from migrationinformation.org

Milagros Santos, R., et al. (2004). Concept Paper: *Responsiveness to family, culture, values and education*. Missoula, MT: Council on Exceptional Children: Division for Early Childhood. Retrieved from dec-sped.org

New American children. (2012). New York: Foundation for Child Development. Retrieved from fcd-us.org/our-work/new-american-children Article is no longer available online.

Olson S. (Ed.). (2011). Demographic perspectives on family change. In *Toward an integrated science of research on families: Workshop report*. U.S. Institute of Medicine and U.S. National Research Council Committee on the Science of Research on Families; Washington, DC: National Academies Press. Retrieved from ncbi.nlm.nih.gov/ books/NBK56255/ Article is no longer available online.

Savarese, R. (2007). *Reasonable people: A memoir of autism and adoption*. New York: Other Press.

Trumbull, E., & Pacheco, M. (2005). *The teacher's guide to diversity: Building a knowledge base*. Brown University. Retrieved from www.brown.edu/academics/education-alliance/publications/teachers-guide-diversity-building-knowledge-base-volume-i-human-development-culture-and

Vandivere, S., Malm, K., & Radel, L. (2009). *Adoption USA: A chartbook based on the 2007 National Survey of Adoptive Parents*. Washington, DC: U.S. Dept of Health and Human Services. Retrieved from https://aspe.hhs.gov/report/adoption-usa-chartbook-based-2007-national-survey-adoptive-parents

Wallman, K. (2012). *America's children in brief: Key national indicators of well-being*. Washington, DC: U.S. Government Printing Office. Federal Interagency Forum on Child and Family Statistics.

WFD Consulting (2004). *A parent's guide to family-friendly child care centers*. Retrieved from childrenscenter.boisestate.edu/wp-content/uploads/documents/family-friendly-care-centers-guide.pdf

Lisa King

Lisa King is the mom in a modern family of seven in Eugene, Oregon. She and her husband are the parents of four (adopted) children, and guardian of one. In addition to managing household schedules, meals, laundry, transportation, and homework, she teaches ESL at Lane Community College.

Kirsten Haugen

Kirsten Haugen is Working Group Coordinator for the World Forum on Early Care and Education and runs an after-school writing and publishing program at edisonlightbulb.edublogs.org. She is the mom in a conventional looking family of four that tends to defy conventions on a regular, but unpredictable, basis.

Hearing Parents in Every Language

An Invitation to ECE Professionals

by Holly Elissa Bruno

How Far Can the Willow Bend?

The wise woman said, "To find your treasure, look in your own backyard." Child care professionals do not have to travel far to find the riches of the world. Children and their families from Afghanistan, Cambodia, China, Romania, Nigeria, Kuwait, Creek and Cherokee nations, urban and countryside America, bring opulent, vibrant, runny-nosed treasures to our programs.

In appreciation of these treasures, we invite each child and her family to be 'at home' in our centers. We want everyone to feel welcome, respected, honored in the richness of her diversity. NAEYC's *Code of Ethical Conduct* reminds us to respect each family's differences.

What happens, however, when one of our core values clashes with the new family's beliefs and practices?

- Kaori's (age 1) mom tells you her daughter must use the toilet.

- Six-year old Amalia sleeps in the same bed with her grandparents.

- Emmaline Rae's dad declares no man is allowed to look at his baby daughter's uncovered body.

- Jinhee's mom appears dispassionate about those deep purple bruises on Jinhee's bottom.

- Mr. Khan instructs you to treat his son like a prince, and his daughter like the obedient wife she is bethrothed to become.

When is the traditional American standard to be upheld? Governing bodies, representing dominant cultures, name what is and is not acceptable. Our courts, for example, uphold English as the language of our classrooms. State licensing regulations mandate standardized behaviors. NAEYC sets developmentally appropriate practices. Each one of us has our own sense of right and wrong. Yet, each child is special.

This article is a gentle invitation for each of us to consider how open we can be to the richness of each child, within the context of professional rules and regulations. Consider how far you can flex to accommodate differences while upholding required standards. How far does the willow bend before it breaks?

Assumptions, Judgments, Wonderment: Ask and Listen

Rules, written or unwritten, lead to expectations for appropriate behavior. When a child of a culture other than my own comes to me, I naturally respond according to my own assumptions.

For example, I expect girls and boys to have a right to the same opportunities. I was raised when girls were shut out of career choices, and boys were not allowed to cry. I have fought for gender equality. Mr. Khan's heritage allows more rights to males than females. He asks if I will treat Amin as a prince, while teaching Roshan obedience. My gut reacts righteously: "Never!" I have no room for wonderment, only judgment. What if instead, I set aside for the moment my assumptions so that I can ASK AND LISTEN to Amin and Roshan's dad? Can I open myself to hear about the traditions, practices, and hopes of this man who differs from me? If I listen in wonderment, might I learn how this father loves his children? That he wants the best for them? That he wants to prepare them for success by the standards of his religious and cultural tradition?

"Ask and Listen" questions are open-ended. Examples include:

- Tell me about your child.

- What activities does your family like to do together?

- What is important to you in raising your child?

- How was your weekend/vacation/afternoon together?

- What are ways your child feels comforted, soothed?

- Is there anything you would like me to know about your child?

If I can ASK AND LISTEN, I may be able to find common ground. I may be able to find that quieter place inside myself where I relax my ego and open myself to wonderment. I 'put to the side' my story that Mr. Khan is sexist, while I listen for ways to partner in support of his children.

In the end, I share with him the philosophy of our program, that we treat each child as precious. I invite him to see if together, we can find a way for Amin and Roshan to feel comfortable in our program, given our differences.

Sitting at the Same Side of the Table

When I think differences can never be bridged, I remind myself of President Jimmy Carter's negotiating a peace agreement between two archenemies. President Carter created a safe, non-judgmental space of wonderment for the leaders of two warring powers, Israel and Egypt, to find common ground. Anwar Sadat and Menachim Begin carried the scars of centuries of jihad. Sadat and Begin did not want to be in the same room, and certainly not at the same side of the table.

Something inspired President Carter to invite each man to talk about his grandchildren. "Tell us about them, what they are like, what they love, what they want to be," encouraged Carter. Slowly the stiffly defended men softened into gentle, beaming grandfathers with endless stories of delight. In the end, leaders Sadat and Begin agreed that the world should be a safer, saner place for their grandchildren than it had been for them. The peace accord was signed. A humble President Carter added his own cultural history in announcing the accord: "In my religious heritage, we say 'blessed are the peacemakers.'"

An ECE professional, by sitting at the 'same side of the table' with a parent from another culture, can be a peacemaker. By looking together for common ground in how we can serve the children, we may in wonderment find ways to honor the cultures we represent.

When the Dominant Culture Prevails

When does the willow bend too far and break? When might valuing differences go too far? At times, our state, federal, and professional standards mandate that we enforce what is right for the majority, while negating the difference of the minority.

For example, every child has been mandated to learn English in this country. The necessity for a common language has meant that children raised with 'minority' languages, have to abandon their primary way of communicating at school. This principle is the same in our profession: for the health and safety of the children, standardized practices prevail.

Universal precautions like hand washing and wearing of plastic gloves are required. Class sizes are mandated. Child abuse and neglect are criminal offenses in America.

By law, we are mandated reporters of abuse. What do we do when a child has puffy red streaks on her back? Some of us immediately file an abuse report with the state. Others talk to the parent first. The parent explains 'coining' is a practice her culture uses to heal a fever. "Look how much better the child is!" answers the proud mom. Do you report abuse?

Remember Jinhee's bruised bottom? Jinhee is my Korean-born daughter's middle name. Mongolian spots polka-dotted her bottom throughout her preschool years until they faded away. Such purple pigmentation is not unusual with Korean children. Her brother Nick's ear lobe still appears bruised. If the observer had failed to ASK AND LISTEN to me as a parent, he may have reported me for abuse.

America has a painful history of denying rights to minority cultures. Recall the injustice done to Japanese-Americans during World War II. Our Supreme Court banished them to camps, leaving behind homes, trust, businesses, and respect. Our country's history of denying human rights to African Americans sadly speaks for itself.

Balancing the need to uphold accustomed ways of the majority, while respecting the unaccustomed ways of the minority, is a dilemma that may always be with us. The 'letter of the law' does not always reflect the 'spirit of the law.'

When we sit at the same side of the table, however, our differences do not divide us. They unite us in facing a common problem. Sadat and Begin peered deep beneath the surface of their differences until they found their common dilemma. They could then sit together on the same side of the table, examine their common problem, and unite on its solution.

The "Ask and Listen" Practice

Here are the steps to asking and hearing. I call this the "wonderment" approach as opposed to jumping-to-conclusions response.

■ **Acknowledge the assumptions I bring to the conversation.** This includes noticing what offends me at a gut level. I assumed Mr. Khan was sexist and wrong.

■ **Set the assumption to the side.** This does not mean I let go of the assumption, even if I could will myself to do so. I name and hold the assumption off to the side, to better hear the other person.

■ **Keep my eyes on the prize of serving children and families.** I choose to learn about the family's practices, beliefs, desires.

■ **Find common ground.** Seek ways in which the parent and I agree to interact with the child.

■ **Name the differences.** Note what the parent and I cannot negotiate.

■ **Review the standards and requirements of laws, regulations, accreditation, program philosophy.** Work together to: a) find ways to honor the difference while acting 'in the spirit of the law,' or b) help the parent find another center that better fits his/her needs.

Eyes on the Prize

Each of the families in the following case studies is worthy of respect. The life experiences and beliefs of some of these families/staff members may differ from your own. As you read these real-life situations, ask yourself:

■ What assumptions might I bring to this situation?

■ How could I "ask and listen" for what the parties desire?

■ At what point, if any, would I feel I must tell the parent/staff member that her/his practice is not acceptable?

Each family's diversity is to be honored. At the same time, state and federal rules and regulations mandate certain standardized practices. What decisions can you make when the individual and the dominant standards do not match?

Case Studies

Kaori — Kaori's parents recently arrived from Japan. Much of Kaori's care has been given by her beloved grandmom, who has just passed away. Grandmom always gently placed Kaori on the baby toilet when grandmom felt Kaori's little body move as if she where ready to go. Mom says Kaori has come to 'know' those feelings inside herself. Kaori's teacher Leah, who has just gotten an A in her developmentally appropriate practices course, is offended that Kaori is being 'forced' to behave this way.

Jinhee — First grader Jinhee is a quiet, cautious child, who doesn't like group activities. Observant Jinhee is quick to learn and try things on her own. She always comes to your after-school program attractively dressed and immaculate. Bruce, the new lead teacher, notices dark purple bruises on Jinhee's back when she wears a halter-top. Jinhee's usual teacher is out for the week. Bruce comes to you to say he must report Jinhee's mom, a single working parent, for abuse.

Tyrone — Tyrone is busy, active, spontaneous, and commanding at age seven. He doesn't like to sit still. He interacts confidently with children and adults of any background. When Tyrone play-acts the daddy, he spanks the boy doll for 'foolishness' and yells he's going to hit that baby "upside the head." Teacher's aide, Rebecca, and team teacher Margaret disagree over what to say to Tyrone's dad. The Anglo teachers fear they might say something offensive to this African American parent.

Amin and Roshan — Mr. Khan chose your program because your brochures say "honoring diversity" is a high priority. He notes your NAEYC accreditation and has read their standards for valuing differences. He wants to enroll his son and daughter, Amin and Roshan. Amin is a prince in his family; Roshan was bethrothed at birth to become one of seven obedient wives of a wealthy man back home. Mr. Khan expects you to respect his culture by helping his children prepare for their future roles.

Amalia — Amalia is a happy, free-spirited, physically loving six year old. She is very close to her mom's family, all of who emigrated from Cuba. Amalia speaks Spanish and English fluidly, often explaining terms to her relatives who come to pick her up. One day, as children are doing a project on their rooms at home, Amalia draws a picture of herself in bed with two adults. She readily tells you she sleeps and snuggles with her grandparents every night. Your team teacher is upset about lack of boundaries and inappropriate exposure to sexuality.

Emmaline Rae — Baby Emmaline Rae's dad, Wilbur, tells her teacher, Luis, that Luis cannot change the baby's diaper. "No man may see my daughter's body, or she will be shamed," Wilbur says. Wilbur is very strong in his fundamentalist religious beliefs about gender roles and modesty. He himself never bathes or changes Emmaline Rae. He relies on his wife, female church and family members, all of whom are strongly supportive. Luis is your best infant teacher, and you are often understaffed.

Scooter — School-aged Scooter adores dressing up. He is willing to wear anything from a frothy wedding dress to an astronaut suit. He likes wrapping long, colorful scarves around his neck to fly around like the Red Baron aviator or Isodora Duncan. You have to work with other children so they won't make fun of Scooter's theatrical ways. Scooter's dad, Ramon, is fiercely supportive of Scooter's individuality. His other dad, Timothy, urges you to "make Scooter learn to fit in better." Timothy and Ramon arrive at pick-up time to find Scooter playing dress-up with all the girls; boys are out playing soccer. Timothy demands you tell Scooter "in no uncertain terms" never to play dress-up again.

Laura — Laura's mom, Mrs. Petrezullio, believes her child is perfect. Every time Laura's teachers attempt to share information about Laura's disruptive behavior, Mrs. Petrezullio insists: "Laura never does that at home; you must be provoking her!" On Monday,

Laura bit Clarence. On Tuesday, Laura punched Josefina in the belly; on Wednesday, Laura refusing to sit with others at circle time, began to pull everyone's belongings out of their cubbies. Laura often swears to herself, making no sense to others. Laura's teachers want Laura to be evaluated; they are afraid of Mom's reaction.

Holly Elissa Bruno

Holly Elissa Bruno, MA, JD, is a best-selling author, international keynote speaker, ground-breaking radio host, and seasoned team builder. She served as Assistant Attorney General for the state of Maine and Assistant Dean at the University of Maine School of Law. An alumna of Harvard University's Institute for Educational Management, she teaches leadership courses for The McCormick Center for Early Childhood Leadership and Wheelock College. Holly Elissa's books include the best-selling, *What You Need to Lead an Early Childhood Program: Emotional Intelligence in Practice* (NAEYC, 2012), *Managing Legal Risks in Ear ly Childhood Programs* (Columbia University's Teachers College Press, November 2012), and *Learning from the Bumps in the Road* (Redleaf Press, 2013). Her first book, *Leading on Purpose*, was published by McGraw-Hill in 2008. To share your story in Holly Elissa's upcoming book on 2nd chances, go to her blog at hollyelissabruno.com. To 'recovering attorney' Holly Elissa, life is too short to do anything but enjoy it daily.

Dialogue to Understanding Across Cultures

by Janet Gonzalez-Mena

Some child care directors and staff are experts at handling two children squabbling; but when tensions arise between themselves and parents, it can be a different story. Conflicts may come up around program policies or maybe it's just a small practical matter like bibs on toddlers. Behind the conflict may be differing notions of what's best for children, or for a particular child. When professionals find themselves in such a conflict with a parent, it's a good idea to ask if this is a cultural conflict.

Sometimes what a parent wants doesn't make any sense to the professional. In that case, professionals have to listen, really listen, to parents. To do that listening, they have to step down from their place of power and put themselves in the role of learner. It's not easy for most professionals to accept that their knowledge has limitations, especially when what the parent is telling them doesn't sound reasonable.

Let's play that out. A parent comes with what seems a small complaint. Her toddler gets food on his clothes.

Her solution: spoon-feed him. The director has a different solution: a bib. Spoon-feeding doesn't make any sense to the director. She talks about the importance of self-help skills, independence, and individuality, then considers the matter finished. The mother smiles, says thank you, and leaves. Problem solved. But is it?

What if the mother has overwhelming concerns about whether her child is being nurtured enough, and the complaint wasn't really about dirty clothes at all? Or what if the mother doesn't believe in independence and individuality? Instead, her goal is interdependence. Spoon-feeding is an important part of that goal because in her mind it creates a closeness that is lacking when children feed themselves.

The smile and the thank you did not indicate that the parent agreed, but were merely social conventions that the parent felt the situation called for. What the director experienced as a small complaint could in reality be a very large cultural difference. Furthermore, the mother's acquiescence to the director's quick solution could be the habitual response of a woman who has experienced a lifetime of oppression. A more privileged and powerful parent might have refused to be dismissed so quickly.

The way to find out these things is to open up an ongoing dialogue. To do that, the professional has to genuinely want to understand the complaint and everything behind it. She has to let the parent know that she will listen and not discount or criticize. The parent may not trust her at first until she proves she is sincere about wanting to understand. If the professional is white and middle class, she needs to also be open to the idea that the power she represents may make it difficult for this mother to trust her. It may take a lot of work at relationship building before a dialogue about important issues can take place.

Part of the dialogue involves taking a good hard look at your own attitudes and biases and realizing that you might have a monocultural viewpoint. You have to be open to seeing the parent's perspective without judging it. You have to tell yourself that the parent is speaking her own truth, even if it is not yours. Ask questions as a way of understanding rather than as a way of trying to convince the other person of your truth.

Let's look at a different kind of situation that needs cross-cultural understanding and knowledge. A Vietnamese child arrives in the morning with bright red streaks on his neck. When his teacher questions him, he explains his mommy 'coined' him. The teacher has never heard of coining and goes to the director who has never heard of it either. Luckily they decide that they need to understand more before picking up the phone and calling the child abuse authorities. When they investigate, they learn that 'coining' is a Vietnamese health measure involving putting a special kind of ointment on the skin and rubbing a coin back and forth.

It may be hard to understand why a health measure doesn't look healthy. But that's an outsider's perspective. Imagine if you moved to a country where they had never heard of immunizations. What would be the reaction to sticking needles in a baby's arm if no one knew about DPT shots? The practice seems abusive if you don't understand it, especially in the face of the resulting red lump on the arm and fever.

Of course, in the name of listening, professionals mustn't throw out judgment entirely or forever. For example, a caregiver in dialogue with a parent of a newborn who is telling her to put her baby to sleep on her tummy would need to say something about the research on Sudden Infant Death Syndrome (SIDS). It's the professional's responsibility to share information about the risk factors of prone sleeping.

What makes conflict situations hard is that most child care practices don't have proven risks. They aren't clearly right or wrong. Differences in practices often depend on differences in priorities, and many of those priorities reflect cultural differences. Sometimes professionals get in a situation where they feel so strongly that they are right that they can't see another view. It takes humility and willingness to see another perspective besides one's own.

Dialoguing is an approach to conflict that is more effective than arguing. Arguing has to do with persuasion — with winning and losing. Dialoguing is different. Rather than trying to convince someone of their viewpoint, people engaged in dialogue try to understand the other perspective. The idea is not to win, but to find the best solution for all concerned. Dialogue levels the playing field and helps the parties in conflict negotiate an agreement without either side *giving in*.

Dissonance is where growth takes place. Professionals need to be able to problem solve in ways that make differences manageable. Some problems can't be solved, in which case both professional and parent need to develop conflict coping skills. Even though harmony may be a goal, it's not a final state but merely a temporary condition. Professionals have to recognize the richness that comes from an environment where there are differences and disagreements. Only when professionals acknowledge that diversity is good, necessary, and provides growth will they be able to effectively respond to children and their families enrolled in early childhood programs. Only when they learn to dialogue effectively will they be able to respond equitably to differences, whether cultural or not.

Janet Gonzalez-Mena

Janet Gonzalez-Mena was a student of Lilian Katz, Magda Gerber, and Anna Tardos. Today she does consulting and training in infant-toddler care, parenting, and diversity work.

Retrato de Mi Familia:

A Portrait of My Hispanic Family

by Rebeca María Barrera

"*Vente mihijita*, say hello to your grandmother first. Now give your *tía* a big hug."

I remember the Sunday rituals so clearly. Sunday was family day, and we visited relatives. It was always this way, with the younger members going to the older person's home, never the other way around. Of course, we were visited occasionally, but never for the Sunday gatherings. I looked forward to playing with my ten cousins.

We'd walk in the front door and smell *caldo* cooking on the stove or *carne asada* being grilled on a fire outside, and our cousins would call us into the kitchen to taste the first hot corn *tortilla*, sprinkled with salt and rolled into a flute. We never made it past the living room before the *tías* caught us for the dreaded ritual — one hug, one kiss per aunt, neighbor, or friend of an aunt. These weren't ordinary aunts. They were the five great aunts of the family, the sisters of my grandmother. Greeting them first was obligatory, and it took forever. In Spanish, we had to detail how we were doing in school, whether we were giving our parents the respect they merited, why our hair was in a ponytail instead of braids, or why we had fought with our brother. They always knew everything, and the interview always made me squirm. *Tía Elia* was the best, though. She usually had a plate of her special muffins, and she always told me I was pretty.

Finally allowed to go outside, we would cluster around the men at the barbecue pit and listen to their stories about cattle, farming conditions, and wildlife around the ranch. If it was someone's birthday, we broke a *piñata*. Before we ate, everyone sampled the food, snitching a taste here and a *tortilla* there. Lavish compliments were declared of all the cooks, and everyone helped set the table, including the little ones who carried napkins to each place. Looking back on these events today, I realize how they capture the essence of our Méxican American heritage. Beginnings and endings are ritualized in our very large families. When a child is born, or a baptism, wedding, or birthday takes place, everyone gathers. The family members bestow their blessings and good wishes personally. Each person has a stake in the life of the celebrated member. This tradition follows throughout life.

Culture is a Family Portrait

These memories, while not obviously early childhood related, are in fact the core of living in a Hispanic family. The interdependence of family members is so essential to family living that, without it, individual members will not thrive. Today's barrio youth coming from unstable families need to feel they belong; instead they join gangs in unprecedented numbers to find the bonding they long for. The need exists also in the preschool environment, where rituals are necessary for children to feel they are welcome and belong.

Culture may be superficially represented by holidays, food, and music; but the deep culture is the one that really counts, and it is the most difficult for a non-member of the culture to understand. The rituals at mealtime, the greetings and good-byes, are all distinctly Hispanic.

Ideas for the Classroom

Making the classroom a comfortable place for children requires incorporating their culture, some of their family rituals and traditions, into the classroom environment. Listed are some ideas:

■ **Learn to pronounce Spanish names; help children develop pride in their name and its Spanish meaning.** Many Hispanics allow others to change the pronunciation because it is easier than having to correct mispronunciation. Experience shows that persons who readily give up the correct pronunciation generally have become acculturated and have lost their identity with their home culture. It is important to maintain a balance between Hispanic and the dominant American culture, but over-acculturation separates children from their elders to whom they can no longer relate comfortably. Mispronunciation of the name is a sign that this has occurred.

■ **Establish rituals for greetings and departures.** Ask children how to acknowledge persons who come to the door, especially older persons.

Children should always greet each other's parents and each other.

■ **Begin the morning each day with a review of home activities from the night before.** Talking about common family experiences is an excellent self-esteem activity.

■ **Let the children work in cooperative play most of the day.** They are accustomed to being in groups. While Hispanic children need some time for individual work, many will consider it a punishment to be separated from the group.

■ **Establish clear boundaries for learning centers, but don't be surprised to find eight children in a small space.** Hispanic families are large, and space is always snug. Don't be compelled to force one child into one space.

■ **Create opportunities for multi-age groupings.** Children in Hispanic families have roles and responsibilities for younger siblings. They are not accustomed to being separated by ages, and the interaction between age groups is essential for normal family care. In multi-age classrooms, older children develop caring skills for younger children. The younger children get more personal attention and look up to role models. Modeling becomes a practical strategy for learning new skills. Family interdependence and responsibility for each other is reinforced.

■ **Plan longer mealtimes.** Sitting at the table and talking is an essential social skill for families. Without an opportunity to practice, children lose the patience and interest needed to sit after finishing eating.

■ **Set up nap mats so that children can whisper to each other until they fall asleep.** In large families children sleep several to a room, sometimes two or three to a bed. They need to be able to reach out and touch each other at naptime. Sometimes teachers confuse this with misbehavior. By emphasizing separation, the teacher may inadvertently be creating anxiety problems.

■ **Teach children to maintain the classroom together.** All Hispanic children are responsible for each other's activities. When a child leaves blocks on the floor, instead of demanding to know who left the blocks and standing over the culprit until the task is complete, ask several children to help clean up. Another day, that child will help them clean up. Eventually they will monitor each other.

■ **Expect children to want to be involved in 'your business.'** At home, they participate in most activities. They are accustomed to attending adult dinners, sports events, weddings, funerals, and even going to work with their parents. At the end of the month, many children accompany their parents from the telephone company to the doctor's office to pay bills for the month. They will feel discounted if they are told something is for adults only. Handle this gently, but set limits.

■ **Keep discipline issues between you and the child unless you absolutely must have parent intervention.** Telling a parent about each little *pecadillo* embarrasses the parent. The interdependency between parent and child is such that the parent will feel personally responsible for the child's action, and will be humiliated by your report that their child misbehaved.

■ Use storytelling as a tool to change behavior or teach a lesson. To get a point across, Hispanic family elders usually intersperse *dichos* and stories in their conversation. *Dichos*, or sayings, are found in most cultures and they carry vital messages about social behavior, values, and societal rules.

■ Gather materials from the home to incorporate into classroom activities. Some examples are:

• wooden *molinillo* for whipping hot chocolate.

• *tortilla press* and rolling pins for cooking activities.

• *molcajete* to grind corn or mash avocados into guacamole.

• herbs and spices for scent activities.

• tairas, hats, flower bouquets, and *quinceañera* veils for dramatic play

• guitar, *maracas, conga* drums and other rhythm instruments.

• Méxican coins for sorting.

• family photos.

• records and tapes with contemporary *Tejano, salsa,* or *cumbia* music.

• *piñatas, baleros,* and other toy items.

• ceramic tiles and tile patterns to match or assemble like a puzzle.

• straw baskets.

• *arpilleras, molas,* weavings, and other traditional artwork.

Ideas for Working with Families

Working with the whole family is essential when working with Hispanic children. Building bridges between home and school is necessary in order to understand the uniqueness of the culture. Listed are some suggestions:

■ **Plan for the whole family to come to parent night.** Child care is essential if you want adult-only discussions, otherwise expect the children to want to sit with their parents. Grandmothers or other relatives will accompany parents.

■ **Interview parents to explore their deep culture.** Ask about special days or traditions. Find out how parents guide behavior. Discuss rewards and how the family recognizes special achievement. Inquire about rites of passage such as taking the first step or losing the first tooth. Inquire about family events. Children will talk about an event for weeks before it occurs. This is part of the normal family preparation for a birth, celebration, or holiday. Also expect a repeat of the story after the event occurs.

- **Always plan food with school events.** Family box suppers or potluck dinners are ideal. Failure to plan for food will indicate poor hospitality and create an unwelcome feeling.

- **Be very conscious of age.** Remember that older persons are revered in Hispanic culture. A grandmother visiting the school has more 'presence' than the mother. Never make conversation that does not include both persons.

- **Expect the unexpected.** There are many things that are personal to families, and their ancient cultures. A comment about *curanderos* (herb healers) is not a suggestion of witchcraft or satanic worship. In past centuries, there were no medical doctors, and the scientists of the village were the persons who understood the medicinal value of certain tea leaves or spices. Avoid making judgments about home remedies.

- **Use storytelling to build bridges.** Ask family members to tell stories about their families. These adventures will be much more relevant than some contemporary picture books. The children need both. Don't be surprised if some of the themes include crossing the border, crossing the Gulf of México by boat, being chased by the *migra* (immigration), or a historical account of the *rinches* (Texas Rangers). Hispanics are a conquered people whose land was acquired by the United States or expropriated by a dictator. There may be painful legends and stories in the family's history.

¿Cuál Idoma?

Language has been a barrier to educational success for Hispanic children. Although this article focuses on the cultural issues, the question of language must not be separated from culture. Teachers and directors who are bilingual will know that there are formal and informal ways to communicate with parents, and that the use of one form implies intimacy and the other implies distance.

There are different words for the same item among Cubans, Méxican Americans, Puerto Ricans, and Spaniards. The variations are even greater when the Central American or South American indigenous languages are mixed. Speaking Spanish may not be enough. Learning the regional differences will become more important as we move toward a global lifestyle.

Despedida

While it is important to teach children about other cultures, this is not the same thing as a culturally relevant classroom. Other cultures are frequently introduced as a theme to be studied — like plants, transportation, or rivers. A teacher who incorporates words and culture from the child's home into the classroom environment is doing much more.

The acceptance of the child's heritage builds a comfort zone; and it releases the talents, skills, and knowledge hidden by the blanket of another culture. The culturally sensitive environment empowers the child to succeed in a way we hope will reverse the 50% dropout rate among Hispanics.

We can all benefit from the freedom we gain as we explore our deepest feelings and values and use the positive energy in our classrooms. As we pass culture to the next generation, we know that some things are lost in the wake of technological advances and mobility. Perhaps the children will remember them through the stories they hear from us.

Rebeca María Barrera

Rebeca Barrera is a cultural translator and bilingual program designer. A lifelong educator, she has worked to infuse cultural understanding into every level of curriculum development from early childhood to university courses. As founder and President of the National Latino Children's Institute, her cultural work focused on non-profit organizations and their effectiveness in serving young Latinos and other minority children. After eight years as Director of Latino Initiatives at Scholastic, Rebeca Barrera is entering the marketplace with her own products and services through her cultural design studio, Tres Rebecas.

Lesbian, Gay, Bisexual, and Transgender (LGBT) Families

Tools for Directors in Supporting Staff Discussion Dealing with Fears

by Tracy Burt and Lee Klinger Lesser

Building a staff team and community that addresses controversial and difficult subjects involves creating space where we can take risks; disagree with and honor each others' perspectives; build strong, authentic relationships; and provide resources and support for ongoing learning. While accomplishing this in the context of supporting LGBT families brings challenges, it also brings opportunities for renewed growth, professional development, and deeper relationships. Engaging in this process strengthens the capacity of educators to fulfill our responsibility to support all children in the context of their families and their own emerging sense of self.

The Importance of Inclusion

One of the first steps is to understand why it is important to engage in this work. The NAEYC *Code of Ethical Conduct* states in Principle 1.1 "Above all, we shall not harm children. We shall not participate in practices that are emotionally damaging, physically harmful, disrespectful, degrading, dangerous, exploitative, or intimidating to children. This principle has precedence over all others in this Code." When a child's family is rendered invisible, the child is harmed.

Silence has a powerful voice, especially when it excludes the people most important to children, the people who keep them safe, and tuck them into bed at night and feed them and love them — their family. Even when it is not the intention of an educator to create harm, it may in fact be the result. An example:

A lesbian mother overheard her second grade daughter, Jenny, and her best friend, Rita, having a conversation in the other room:

Jenny: "I hate having two moms!"

Rita: "Why?"

Jenny: "I hate it when the teacher says 'Take this home to your mom or dad.'"

The educator involved probably had no idea that her words would impact Jenny this way. Through our everyday actions and language in the classroom, we convey messages of acceptance or rejection, of 'normalcy' or strangeness that teach a child whether or not they are welcomed, valued, and included in this world. Jenny was given the message that she and her family didn't belong.

The silence and invisibility about LGBT people in early childhood settings lays the foundation for the harassment that begins in elementary school and leads to bullying, violence, and teen suicide. Some of the most common insults used by children on the playground beginning in elementary school are 'gay' or 'faggot.' These are often words that children do not even understand, and yet are allowed to use in derogatory ways without adult intervention. The Yes Institute, a non-profit organization dedicated to preventing youth suicide, provides the following statistics:

- 33% of all teen suicides are lesbian and gay youth.

- 50% of lesbian and gay youth are rejected by their own families when their sexual orientation is disclosed.

- 80% of youth harassed as gay actually identify as heterosexual, and are five times more likely to commit suicide than other youth.

- 97% of high school students hear anti-gay epithets.[1]

There is at least one child in almost every early childhood classroom who in later years will recognize their identity as lesbian, gay, bisexual, or transgender. Silence, fear, negativity, or avoidance about LGBT people in educational settings gives them the message that they are neither welcome nor safe in this world.

Even around a topic that is so emotionally and politically charged, when an opportunity is provided, most people are eager to explore their own fears and beliefs along with their desire to provide the best care they can to children and families.

Opening the Dialogue

Addressing issues related to LGBT parenting is complex: personal religious conflicts, safety for LGBT staff, and lack of experience talking about the issues are often layered upon discomfort with conflict and/or lack of experience negotiating conflict successfully with colleagues. Creating room for dialogue and allowing space for people to wrestle with their own dilemmas is fundamental.

Listed are some strategies that help to open and sustain dialogue:

Set the Context — Begin with this shared core belief: We want to do what is best for the children.

Acknowledge everyone's commitment to serving the children in their care. Honor every person's right to their own beliefs, and invite people to consider other perspectives. Relate your conversations about supporting gay and lesbian families to your mission and philosophy.

Open Conversations Thoughtfully — Acknowledge that it can be difficult to talk about topics that we feel strongly about and also that you are committed to ongoing dialogue. Introduce the topic by connecting your support of lesbian, gay, bisexual, and transgender families with your commitment to fully serving all families and honoring the fact that everyone enters this conversation from a different place.

Be Prepared — Collect some articles with information about LGBT families including research and resources for early childhood curriculum. We recommend "Belonging: Including Children of Gay and Lesbian Parents — and All Children — in Your Program" (Gelnaw, 2005) and Lesbian and Gay Parenting by the American Psychological Association (2005).

Ask Questions — Help people explore and ask questions about their own practices. What is the impact of children learning that they don't belong? If children learned to accept LGBT families, how might that later impact bullying and violence?

Tie Your Conversations Back to Practice — Ask: "How does what you learned today relate to your interactions with children and families? What will you do differently?"

Common Fears and Strategies to Address Them

Below we list common fears and concerns of educators, along with strategies to work with each of them:

I want to do this but don't know how. *Practice Reading LGBT Inclusive Children's Books.* Bring several children's books to a meeting and read one to your staff. Invite them to pretend to be children and to ask the questions they are afraid children or parents might ask them. Model how you would respond to the questions and take turns practicing reading books and answering the questions. Support staff to begin reading books in their classroom.

Explore the implications of Mother's Day and Father's Day Celebrations on children who do not have (or live with) a mother or a father. Use the article "What Mother? What Father?" (Lewis, 1996) to stimulate discussion. How can you ensure that all children and families are included in your celebrations?

Brainstorm curriculum ideas. Create activities that include LGBT families for all aspects of the environment and curriculum. Support staff to begin implementing new curriculum at the level to which they are ready. A simple way to enhance curriculum is to adapt common children's songs with new words that describe the diversity of families. Some examples of these songs developed by different educators are available at www.parentservices.org.

Charles and Milo were looking for a preschool for their three-year-old, Otto. On Wednesday, their friends (a straight couple), toured a prominent preschool and were offered a place in the program right away. When Charles and Milo toured the school on Thursday, they were told that someone would get back to them soon. They were not offered a spot. The next day they heard from their day care provider that the director of the preschool had called her to ask questions about their parenting, and to find out whether Otto seemed happy having two fathers. When the director called them to offer them a spot, they declined. This school, that had come so highly recommended, had one standard for accepting children with straight parents and a separate one for a child with two gay fathers. It was not a reassuring or welcoming place to leave their child.

I don't understand or feel comfortable working with LGBT families. Share Stories. Find stories about real people that will help staff understand the impact of bias on LGBT families. An example:

Invite LGBT parents to share stories with your staff. Show films, such as *Both My Moms' Names are Judy, De Colores, All God's Children, Straight from the Heart,* and *That's a Family.*

Partner with families. Work with LGBT and straight parents to open dialogue and to build a community commitment to support all children and families. Create opportunities to share your mission and commitment with families and to hear their perspectives, questions, and ideas.

I won't be supported by the administration if a parent complains about LGBT inclusive curriculum. *Assess your mission statement and forms.* As a director, it is important to ensure your mission statement explicitly acknowledges your support for LGBT families and that your forms are inclusive. Use the story Forms Loom Large by Kaila Compton, M.D., Ph.D., a lesbian mother who describes the impact on her family of forms that have no room for them (free to download at www.parentservices.org).

Someone will say I am gay if I support LGBT families. *Express your support.* Let your staff know that you will back them up when they include LGBT families in their curriculum. If they are uncomfortable or unsure about how to respond to a question, they should be welcome to refer a parent to you.

Provide support for straight allies. Straight allies are very important in the struggle for the inclusion of LGBT families. Part of what an ally may experience is 'suspicion' of being gay. Provide space for staff to talk about this experience and brainstorm how they would like to respond.

This is against my religious and personal values. *Acknowledge everyone's right to their own beliefs along with the core commitment to fully value every child in your care.* Honor each person's right to their own belief system and also their commitment to serving families. Each individual family has the right to choose what they teach at their home. When we come together in community we are charged with reconciling diverse beliefs and creating acceptance for everyone.

If I talk about gay or lesbian families as normal, it will encourage children to be gay. *Share information.* When we include LGBT families, we are reflecting the diverse sexual orientations and gender identities that exist now and have existed throughout history. The American Psychological Association states "most people experience little or no sense of choice about their sexual orientation" (2008, p. 2). Studies show that extensive prejudice, discrimination, and invisibility cause serious negative effects on health and well-being for LGBT people (Ibid.). As educators, we do not get to choose a child's family or a child's identity. What we can choose is whether we support a child so he or she can thrive.

The story, *On Being a Gay Five Year Old* by Brian Silveira, is a powerful tool to help educators explore this topic (free download, www.parentservices.org).

I don't know how to answer questions from children and parents. *Provide time for role plays and practice.* People are often nervous about answering questions from both children and adults. Give people a chance to practice with adults (or use yourself as a model). Remember, it's not about doing it 'right,' but about practicing your response, and getting feedback from others.

Practice with Scenarios. Use scenarios with staff to explore and uncover their differing beliefs and perspectives. Scenarios for staff training can be downloaded free from www.parentservices.org.

I am afraid that talking about LGBT families means we will be talking about sex. *Clarify.* We are talking about families, not sex. When we talk to children about mothers and fathers, no one thinks we are talking about sex. It is not different when we are talking about mommies and mommies or daddies and daddies. We are talking about families — the people who care for their children, take them to school, change their diapers, and comfort them when they are sad.

Provide information. Many stereotypes and myths exist about LGBT families. It is important to provide accurate information. *Lesbian and Gay Parenting*, published by the American Psychological Association in 2005, reviews extensive research and cogently addresses the most common myths and stereotypes.

I am against 'special rights' for LGBT people. *Share information.* Marriage confers over 1,000 federal and state rights to people who have the right to marry. Many states prohibit second parent adoption, which can have devastating impacts on a child. For example, a lesbian couple, Alma and Diane, lived in a state where only one parent could legally adopt their child. They were partners for eleven years and Alma adopted their eight-year-old son, Jeremiah, as a baby. Diane was the parent who stayed at home and provided more of the day-to-day care. One day, Jeremiah had severe pains and she rushed him to the emergency room. Because Diane had no legal status in relation to Jeremiah, the hospital would not allow her to accompany him when the doctors were examining him. He was terrified and in addition to being in severe pain with a ruptured appendix, he was left alone with strangers and taken away from his mother. Finally, the doctors saw that this was creating more harm for his health and went out to get Diane.

Many people do not realize the impact on children. Without these protections, children are left more vulnerable.

In opening up this topic with your staff, make sure to have a plan that includes dialogue, action, and follow-up. Allow enough time and numerous occasions to explore people's fears and to provide support and information. This is not a one-time conversation or discussion. It takes time to build trust, to explore our own attitudes, and to create new practices with colleagues and families. Each real conversation that we have can help to change lives and to prevent suffering for many children and families.

Bibliography

American Psychological Association. (2008). *Answers to your questions: For a better understanding of sexual orientation and homosexuality*. Washington, DC: Author. Retrieved from www.apa.org/topics/lgbt/orientation.pdf

American Psychological Association. (2005). *Lesbian and gay parenting*. Washington DC: Author. Retrieved from www.apa.org/pi/lgbt/resources/parenting.aspx

Compton, K. (2005). "Forms Loom Large," from *Making Room in the Circle: Lesbian, Gay, Bisexual, and Transgender Families in ECE Settings*. Retrieved from www.parentservices.org Article is no longer available online.

Gelnaw, A. (May/June 2005). "Belonging: Including Children of Gay and Lesbian Parents — and All Children — in Your Program." *Exchange, 163*, 42-45.

Lesser, L., Burt, T., & Gelnaw, A. (2005). *Making room in the circle*. San Rafael, CA: Parent Services Project.

Lewis, E. G. (March 1996). "What Mother? What Father?" *Young Children, 51*(3).

Silveira, B. (2005). "On Being a Gay Five Year Old" from *Making Room in the Circle: Lesbian, Gay, Bisexual, and Transgender Families in ECE Settings*. Retrieved from www.parentservices.org Article is no longer available online.

www.includingallfamilies.blogspot.com
Resources for early childhood educators committed to supporting children and families across gender and sexual orientation.

Endnotes

1 Yes Institute Statistics
   www.yesinstitute.org/resources

Tracy Burt and Lee Klinger Lesser

Together the authors have shepherded hundreds of early childhood educators through short- and long-term dialogues and learning about supporting LGBT (lesbian, gay, bisexual, and transgender) families in early childhood settings. They developed the first three-unit college course in the country on the topic and co-authored the curriculum: *Making Room in the Circle: Lesbian, Gay, Bisexual, and Transgender Families in Early Childhood Settings*. Tracy Burt, EdM., teaches at City College of San Francisco in the Child Development and Family Studies Department. Lee Klinger Lesser, M.S., is the Project and Training Manager for Parent Services Project.

Parents the Second Time Around

by Linda Carlson Johnson

The twin boys, now 5, have never known their mother; she died shortly after their birth. Since then, the boys have lived with their father and his mother. Suddenly, their dad committed suicide, leaving the boys' grandmother with sole responsibility for their care.

At The Right Place, a Salvation Army-operated school readiness center in Hartford, Connecticut, the teachers know right away that something is wrong. The boys seem resentful of everyone, even other children. At naptime, one of the twins says, "Nobody likes me. I hate this world, and I want to die."

Talhaht Mannan, director of The Right Place, knows that this is a tough situation, but, she says, "I already have a plan for this grandmother." Mannan knows a great deal about her: she doesn't have a job, a high school diploma, or a family support system. And she's overwhelmed by her new responsibility.

Before he died, the woman's son wasn't a very reliable parent; he was often out of the picture. But when his mother needed a break, she could call on him and say, "Take your sons and go." No more.

"Now she has nobody to turn to," Mannan says. But she's not ready to give her grandchildren up to anyone else. When Mannan suggested that the twins might be better off placed with a family, the grandmother said, "Oh, my God, how could I do that?"

So Mannan's plan is to find this newly single parent some practical help.

"We need to help get her back together," says Mannan, "to help her get education and training" so she can find a good paying job.

The twins have started half-day kindergarten, but the grandmother would prefer to have them in care at The Right Place all day. Mannan tells her a full day's care won't be possible, but she says the boys can come to the center after school until 5 pm.

Cheerleading for Grandparents

An important part of Mannan's plan for this grand-mother is a large dose of encouragement. That's necessary because, like many grandparents taking on this second-time-around parenting role, this grand-mother feels that she failed her own children — and fears failing her grandchildren, too.

"We want to say to her, 'It's commendable for you to take on this role,'" Mannan says. "And we want to be there to help." At The Right Place, which serves 139 children in the School Readiness program (ages 3-5) and an after-school program called Girls, Inc., about 20% of the children are from homes where a grand-parent — almost always a grandmother — is the primary caregiver.

Mannan says she is glad to be connected to The Salvation Army because of its mission of serving others and because of the many Army programs that are available, such as the Family Center and the Second Time Around program at a Senior Center just a block from the daycare center.

At The Right Place, it's hard to tell from a child's behavior whether the primary caregiver is a parent or grandparent. That's because, in inner-city Hart-ford, one of the poorest cities in the nation, most children arrive with behavioral challenges. "With TV and video games and the culture around them . . . children are exposed to things they are not ready to absorb or understand," Mannan says. "This can lead to children who are aggressive, challenging, strong-willed."

On the Family Plan

For many of these children's parents, and grandpar-ents taking on a primary role in rearing children, Mannan says that for the caregivers of these children, including grandparents, "The economy is just not working for them. They are strapped, undereducated, and low-income. Many are holding down two jobs."

To help, The Right Place has an individual plan for each child — and that child's family. As part of The

Hartford Foundation for Public Giving's Child Care Enhancement Project, The Right Place uses *The Creative Curriculum®* (Teaching Strategies, 2003), which involves intensive training for teachers to help them with the behaviors they encounter in children and to engage parents in the educational process.

"We do parent intake to assess individual needs," says Mannan. "We organize parenting events on a once-a-month basis; we work with high school dropouts to get their GEDs; and if they are not working, we help them find a job. . . . In the long run, if a parent gets more education or a higher paying job, the child has more stability, is more comfortable, and has a sense of belonging."

That's something all children need. But for children being raised by grandparents, the need is all the more acute, because the children often have been trauma-tized very early in life. According to the American Academy for Pediatrics, grandparents come into the picture as caregivers when the children's parents divorce, die, or become disabled; when a teenage daughter has a child and can't or won't take respon-sibility; or when parents are abusive, ill with HIV/AIDS, incarcerated, or abusing alcohol or other drugs.

Surviving Guilt Trips

For grandparents facing the challenge of raising chil-dren all over again, the guilt and burden can seem overwhelming.

"At first, I felt responsible," says Ruth Masters, who is raising her twin grandsons in a sandwich family that includes her own mother as part-time caregiver and a grown son (not the children's father) living in the house. "I wondered what I did wrong that my child would not raise the kids. . . . When you raise your kids, you think that you'll have a perfect little family, and they will grow up to raise their own perfect little family. You can feel so alone as a grandparent with kids."

Over time, Masters has come to grips with her guilt. "Now I feel as if I made mistakes, but I can't blame myself for what my child didn't do. It's in the boys' best interest to be with me."

In Pittsburgh, Pennsylvania, social worker Gloria Luten started a God-Sent Grandparents support group when she noticed an increasing number of grandparents requesting holiday assistance. She had investigated and found that many of the grandparents who were raising their grandchildren were also facing health problems, financial difficulties, and often, tremendous guilt over their children's failure as parents.

Richard and Margaret Allen, who both have jobs, are raising their granddaughter in Connecticut. Both of the girls' parents are alcoholics; but the Allens hope that one day soon, the mother will finish rehab and take custody of her daughter.

"I have no hope at all that that will happen," says Linda Vega. "[My daughter] lives only 15 minutes from me, but the only time she sees [her two children] is when I force them on her. When she does have them, she just sits them in front of the TV. She's 31. The little one has ADHD; the older one is hyperactive and very insecure. She just about made it through first grade. Neither one of them has seen their dad since they were a year or two old." Vega's daughter, now 32, has kicked her drug and alcohol habits, but she has expressed no interest in taking the two children back. One of the children, a girl, is in counseling because she is so angry with her mother. "As she gets older, she gets angrier," says Vega.

Betty Hardy, who is raising her five-year-old granddaughter, says that she recently got a call from school to come in and talk about the girl's aggressive behavior. Hardy, a lead teacher at The Right Place, says that her granddaughter still feels angry at her mother for leaving her with her grandmother.

Danger of Heartbreak

When children live with grandparents, the custody situation can change suddenly, and that can affect both children and grandparents. Peg (last name withheld), who took custody of her granddaughter at age 3, had to give her up at age 12 when she went back to live with her mother. "I was heartbroken; it was like a death," Peg says.

Shifting custody can also be an issue for caregivers in child care centers. If a child, from infancy, knows no other parent than the grandparent, Mannan says, the child will tend to have a sense of stability. But when children move from parents to grandparents, she says, "They are resentful, even of their peers. They say things like, 'I hate everybody.' They become reserved and won't participate. They feel rejected and abandoned by parents."

So what's a caregiver to do? A few suggestions:

- Talk to the grandparent, at intake, about a child's situation. Keep checking in to see how it is working out.

- Provide referrals, as needed, to support groups, mental health professionals, social agencies, legal assistance, and clergy. One place to start is the Grandparents Information Center sponsored by AARP.

- Work with grandparents on establishing consistent discipline at home and school. Grandparents who were expecting to be nurturers, not disciplinarians, for their grandchildren, may need assistance in setting consistent limits.

- Encourage grandparents and provide them with much needed breaks. During December, for example, The Right Place opened in the evening so grandparents, knowing their grandchildren were in a safe place, could feel relaxed about going on an evening shopping trip. Another outing that month was for dinner and a movie.

- Involve grandparents in children's learning. Many grandparents feel intimidated or at a loss when it comes to education, either because of their own lack of schooling or the years of distance since their last school experience.

- Develop a plan for each child that includes the grandparent. Meet with grandparents on a regular basis to ensure that the plans are working for their grandchildren.

Grandmother Ruth Masters says that in a perfect world, her grandsons would not be with her. "But they are, and I believe that's where they need to be," she says. Being a parent all over again, she says, is "hard at times, but it's got its rewards."

For Talhaht Mannan, The Right Place director, the work of a child care center is not just confined to the children, parents, and grandparents she serves. "We want to better [children's] lives. If they receive a quality early childhood education, they won't fall behind or drop out of school, they will stay out of crime, and they will do well at raising their own children. These are the long-term benefits to good early child care." She says her job-satisfaction quotient is very high.

"I've never felt as rewarded as I do here. This is truly serving the community."

Resources

American Academy of Child & Adolescent Psychiatry, at The Grandparents Information Center at the American Association of Retired Persons (2004). Web site: www.AARP.org Article is no longer available online.

DeNavas-Walt, C., Proctor, B. D., & Mills, R. J. (2004). "Income, Poverty, and Health Insurance Coverage in the United States: 2003," pp. 60-226." Washington, DC: U.S. Census Bureau.

The Foundation for Grandparenting, California Communication Center, 108 Farnham Rd., Ojai, CA 93203. Website: http://grandparenting.org

Kinship Care Project Overview (1999). Lansing, MI: Michigan State University School of Social Work.

Resources for grandparents: A guide to relatives caring for children, Second Edition (Fall 2002). Baltimore, MD: Maryland Department of Aging. Website: www.mdoa.state.md.us

"Teaching Strategies Newsletter," Issue 45, Nov. 1, 2004, Teaching Strategies, Inc. (Contains information on *The Right Place, The Creative Curriculum® for Infants & Toddlers and The Creative Curriculum for Preschool®*). Website: www.teachingstrategies.com

"Through the Eyes of a Child: Grandparents Raising Grandchildren," #B3786-4 (2003). University of Wisconsin- Extension, Cooperative Extension, in cooperation with the U.S. Department of Agriculture and Wisconsin counties. This fact sheet is part of a series. Website: http://fyi.uwex.edu/grandparenting/through-the-eyes-of-a-child/

Grandparents Count

- 4.5 million children are living in grandparent-maintained homes. In 1970 that was true for only 2.2 million children.

- 2.4 million children are living in homes where a grandparent has primary responsible for child care.

- 1.9 million of the children are living in households with incomes at or above the poverty line.

- Grandparents raising grandchildren range in age from their 30s to their 60s and beyond. Nearly half are between the ages of 50 and 65.

- Most single grandparents raising grandchildren are women.

Figures: U.S. Census Bureau

Luella Pipkin, 67, has been responsible for the care of more than 30 of her grandchildren at one time or another.

Linda Carlson Johnson

Linda Carlson Johnson is editor-in-chief for Salvation Army publications in the Northeast. She has a B.A. in English from Roanoke College in Virginia and an M.A. from Hartford Seminary. A journalist for more than 20 years, she also taught high school and middle school English. For nine years, she was an editor at *Weekly Reader* and is author of eight books for the school library market.